To darling c
with hug
and apprea
gift you are on the planet
Melissie

What the Seeker Found

Melissie Jolly

ISBN-13: 978-1507893845

ISBN-10: 1507893841

Cover art by Hettie Saaiman - www.hettiesart.com

Editing by Korani Connolly - www.korani.net

Book design by Leila Summers – www.spread-the-word.co.za

Printed in the United States of America

Acknowledgements

This book would never have been attempted if not for Korani Connolly. Without her help, insistence and assistance, not one word would have appeared. Her knowledge and loving encouragement got the project started and finished. Her support was freely and generously given on a daily basis. Korani was the guiding light who sometimes pushed and sometimes gently pulled and was there every step of the way and really, every word of this book is a collaboration. From my scattered thoughts to my scattered English, Korani had to contain and edit it all along the way. She had to herd and corral as if I were a spooked horse to get me to sit down and do this. All the honour really belongs to her and with great love, I thank her from the bottom of my heart. Thank you to my dear friend of longest standing, the artist Hettie Saaiman who created the cover painting. Thank you also to Leila Summers for the book design and for assisting with the publishing process.

Contents

The Personal Questions: All About 'Me'

The People Questions: Human Relationships

The Money Questions

Ascension: Growing In Consciousness

And Finally...

Asking Questions: Becoming a Seeker

Every life has a profound reason for happening. There is no life that is without value or purpose, but for many years I had no idea what on earth mine might be. My early life included a lot of intense and difficult experiences which at the time were bewildering and fairly hideous, but I recognise now that they laid the foundations for my lifelong adventure as a seeker.

I was born on a farm in Kenya just before the Mau Mau revolution into a time of intense fear and turmoil. After my father's entire dairy herd was mutilated in an attack on our farm and he had to shoot them all, we took what we could pack into a car and left East Africa, settling in a small village in the Cape among beautiful blue mountains with a river that ran through the village. It should have been idyllic but as an empath of sorts all I could feel was my father's despair about what he had left behind and I had a miserable time. I was also busy surviving my own revolution – the one inside my body. I had amoebic dysentery that remained undiagnosed for many years, which meant that I had a very tenuous hold on life until the age of 14 when a doctor finally diagnosed and cured it with a series of Emetine injections which were harsher than the disease itself. Right up to the last minute it was not clear whether the disease or I would survive, but I not only survived, I grew up, got married, had children, got divorced – all the usual stuff of life. Like everyone I had my share of struggles, but the challenges I faced helped me to discover at a very deep, true level what I was to learn and teach in the years ahead. I was not going to find my learning only in colleges and universities and books. I was going to have to live it.

My father was a seeker of spiritual truth and consequently opened the door for me to search for truth. We had discussions lasting long into the night and during these conversations I would say to him, "If I die before you, you have to be happy for me because then I will know how it all works." He told me that children were not allowed to die before their parents. I made a deal with him, "If you die before me, you have to come back and tell me how it all works." He laughingly agreed and true to his word, about five months after he died, he suddenly appeared to me – not as the old sick man who had died but as he was when he was young, in a check shirt and shorts with a shock of bright blonde hair. He told me many things but the most important piece of information was that we are so multi-levelled that when we die the ones left behind in their physical heaviness are the only ones who feel

the separation. For those who have passed on, everyone th
have ever loved is right there with them. There is no separation
for them. They completely know we are all one and that love
keeps on existing through time and space. I told him I missed
him anyway and jokingly said that I also missed his cheque
book a lot, and he gave me a slightly sideways look and said he
was working on it. My business and my life's work began quite
soon after that.

At the age of 42 my life found a shape and a form and I
stepped into my service and my joy as I discovered the
wonders of colour and began to work as a colour therapist and
teacher. To everyone who is wondering what it is you are here
for, I would say start with service and joy follows very closely
on its heels. There is no other way that I have discovered. I
remember so clearly one day sitting with a client who was
transforming in front of my eyes and I felt a strange bubble in
my solar plexus. It became so intense that I thought it might be
a heart attack when suddenly I realised that the completely
unfamiliar feeling was... joy!

How often are we surprised by joy? In our busy lives there is
so little room for it and yet it is the most important component
of what we are moving towards. Ascension, the raising of our
vibration to a place of enlightened living, is a by-product of

. There is simply no other way to get there. The only way to really get to heaven on earth is to feel that bubble in the solar plexus of excitement and joy and to be like a small child who looks at the world with excitement and awe at all the wondrous new things there are to discover. I remember being at a workshop at a time when I was really stepping into knowing myself as Divine and even beginning to think I might be a healer. The person running the workshop asked me to stand in front of a crowded room and show them energetically who I was and because she was very psychic and clear I was expecting her to say, "Wow, you are a global healer" and what she said was, "Oh, you only came to have fun." At the time I was shattered but I completely get that actually, they are the same thing and also that it is exactly what I came to do because it is the only possible way to get to the higher vibration that makes Ascension possible.

My life has been a journey where faith has been the only way forward. The right person has always appeared at the right time and the right place has always been created. I have to take a deep breath and chide myself now in those moments when I have the cheek to be worried. Why would I need to do that when every step has been so perfectly laid out without any planning or doing on my side? For a very long time on this planet we set out to learn only through struggle. I believe that one of the shifts that is happening on the Earth at this time is that we are lifting to a vibration where we will no longer have to grow only through pain. We will be part of such a light vibration that any change in the vibration will move everyone and we will no longer have to singly go through all the pain we have had to in the past to move us to the next level in our development.

We started as light and then we had to forget that for a while so that we could fully engage with this life that felt so other, so not the light, and in that forgetting we were gathering information that would add to the knowledge the Allness had of itself as we were adding to our own pool of information. I chose a life path that led to all the experiences I needed, in a family that were everything I had asked them to be, so that I could do the work I came to do. All I have really been asked to do is to show up and in reality, which is all every one of us is asked to do in each moment. Show up for the moment in which you find yourself. Be present in that precise moment and I promise, miracles will happen. They certainly did for me.

I have been working with colour for over 20 years and it has never ceased to bring me joy and deep gratitude. I know without doubt that I had to go through all of the difficulties in order to come to the place of profound peace and plenty that is my life now. I live in Stanford in the Western Cape, a sleepy little town at the foot of the Klein River Mountains. I spend my time running my company, Colour Mirrors, manufacturing coloured oils and essences that have now spread their rainbows worldwide, creating incredible joy for me and a wonderful tool for healing.

So how did I come to write a book? For no reason that makes any sense – except that it makes perfect sense – I have somehow found a life's work that includes the teaching of some spiritual truths and I say that with my tongue firmly in my cheek. I have no real love for 'truth' as a concept. Truth is what every person sees in the moment. There are great Universal Truths, and even those that science can mostly disprove with time, so truth for me has always been a very loose concept. I joke that my mother once gave me a hiding for telling the truth and that has set me free to never really have to worry about it again. I was also young in the 60's when Bob Dylan sang about a man who could not speak but only flatter and I have always rather wished that everyone was like that. I never saw anything but damage come from people who claimed to 'only ever speak the truth'. It seemed to me that truth was always used as a sledgehammer and rarely in a kind way. Truth is so often just a mind concept. The moment you involve your heart, it always feels as if truth is so much more accessible than if you only try and think about it. When you feel into it, when you feel what it is the other person really wants from you, you will know that they very rarely want to be slugged over the head with 'The Truth'. They just want to know that they are acceptable. Perhaps truth is really just love.

Quite often in the last 20 years people have asked me to write a book but one of the things that I have always believed is that I am not a writer. I was deeply dyslexic, dyspraxic and ADD as a child and the moment I am asked to write anything all those old feelings of uselessness come flooding back and I feel quite paralysed. The whole idea of sitting down and writing a book truly terrified me, but I had reckoned without my friend Korani Connolly's gifts of persuasion. When I asked her if she would write the book for me, she politely refused and continually told me I could do it myself. I couldn't see how. I told her that faced with a blank page I feel as if I know nothing, but that if someone asks me a question, somehow the answer always falls into my head. I can speak much more easily than I can write. So, being something of a little terrier and unable to put the idea down, Korani arrived at my door in Stanford all the way from beautiful Wiltshire, England, armed with a recording device and said, "If you need questions, I will ask you questions. We'll record what happens and get it transcribed and there will be the basis of your book."

A list of questions began to form. Some were those we'd asked ourselves, many were those we'd been asked by others, some were suggestions from friends and some were straight out of our imaginings but somehow felt as if they needed to be included. The responses then proceeded to arrive in a most astonishing way with an energy and a power that surprised us both. The end result is a book about 'life, the Universe and everything' and although these questions are only a very few of the many you may ask yourself, what we know is that all the questions and answers it carries act as reminders for those who read it, of the infinite light they carry within. Nothing in this book is 'truth'. Everything is a trigger to get you to connect with your own wisdom and the information your spirit holds for you. This is not a book to sit down and read cover to cover. It is something to be kept to hand and dipped into when you feel called to it. Use it whenever you feel the need for an answer from the Universe or just allow the energy to fill you and connect you with your own wisdom. You do have all the answers inside you. This book is simply a means to help you access them.

What the Seeker Found: Answers

It seems to be part of the human condition to seek, but why would that be? Mostly because you have forgotten who you are and where to find your truth. Often because you have sought experiences at a soul level that have required you to forget so that you could explore and discover and learn. Sometimes simply because you love the thrill of this incredible game.

If you are a seeker, you have probably travelled many paths and had adventures and experiences along the way. In your seeking you will have found things which resonated for you and others which did not feel true for you at all. Some teachings will have struck a 'yes' chord within you while others left you with an underlying sense of dissatisfaction and sent you back to your seeking.

This book is an energy which, as you read, will light up your cells so that the knowledge you already hold within will come streaming through. In truth, you are asking questions not to find answers, but to reactivate the light within you, the true light which fear has kept you from fully knowing and living. As you reactivate that light within, as your light expands, fear has no choice but to dissipate and dissolve and as it does, you find yourself living more and more from light and from the place of love inside you.

This book is a reminder for you as a seeker that the truth always lives within you. It is offered with love and the wish that it might help you remember who you really are, what you're really here for and how and why you exist at this time, in this place.

The Universal Questions

Who am I?

This is an age-old question. The simple answer, the true answer, is that you are a soul, focusing through a human body, having an experience, pretending to be human while being Divine. You are God in a body. When that truth becomes your whole knowing and being you will have reached a place beyond duality, a place of mystic bliss, a place that every spiritual seeker looks for. This is the end of the seeking, the beginning and the end of the journey. There is no need to meditate in a cave for forty years. There is no need to play Mother Teresa. This one question, taken to its ultimate level, leads to enlightenment.

In very simple terms, the answer to this question could actually be the answer to all of the questions in this book, but humans are complex beings with complex lives and ask many questions from many different angles. The rest of this book will explore some of these questions, but as you read, keep this one to the forefront of your mind.

What is the purpose of life?

In truth, there is no purpose. The Allness – what you might call God or Source or All That Is – has never had a purpose except to exist, knowing itself to be Divine. From the blissful infinite knowingness of the Allness, however, a question arose: "How would it be if I didn't know of my own existence? What would it be like to not know?" The Allness, being the ultimate creator, creates with every thought, so with that thought the essence of the Allness split off into individuated sparks which swirled themselves down from the light of the One into dense physicality to experience what it would be to not know. Souls became separate so they could feel separate and in the separation, forget about the Oneness.

You came into being as a human in a body to have a journey with forgetting. In this way, you and all the individual sparks could take that information – what it was to not know that you are Divine – back to the Allness and the Allness would know what it was to be unaware of its own existence. You pretended to be separate and pretended not to be powerful. You chose to be in ignorance of the truth about yourself to see if you could find your way back to the Allness despite not remembering that you were already the Allness. The game was to go out into the world asleep, unaware of your true essence and to find a way back to conscious awareness of yourself as Divine. You pretended to forget and now you are remembering again and in the gathering of that information you are adding to the knowledge the Allness has of itself and because 'as above so below', whatever the Allness develops and evolves into, you become and whatever you develop and evolve into, the Allness becomes.

The reason you exist is simply to exist, but if there is a purpose to life, it is to experience the fullness of everything, to experience emotions and thoughts and plans and deeds, to experience the game and to experience this place you created. The planet is as much an illusion as you are, so in each moment you can set a whole new array of circumstances in motion. You are the master of your Universe and if it pleases you to have a purpose you can decide what it is and be that or do that and create as much fun with it as you wish. You are Shakespeare and you are writing the play that you are living out right now. In every moment you can decide to make your play a comedy or a love story or a tragedy. It is truly up to you.

You know this on some level yet even though you are a master and a creator, there are occasions and situations in your life when you forget this, usually because of the notion of time. With time as the backdrop to your life, you have a body that needs food and clothing and a home and money and you believe that you have to be part of 'consensus reality' in which days pass, bodies age, and life is just a race to stop yourself from dying. The moment you lift yourself above that 'reality' you will see a bigger picture and that picture is an amazing dance of perfection. You will hear the music that plays the Universe and the sound that you are part of which allows you to create so magnificently, because life is sound and colour and beauty and mathematical precision. When you fully know the truth of that, your question about purpose becomes redundant.

Your question comes from the part of you that is the smallest particle in the body of the whole being, the cell in the blood that moves seemingly randomly through the body. You are given thousands of clues about the nature of the Universe. Look at the body as a microcosm of the macrocosm. It is the most astonishingly intricate piece of engineering and the Universe runs exactly as the body does. There is not one random cell in the whole structure. Every single one is on purpose and on track to do what it was meant to do and that is exactly how the Universe operates. Every small particle is in place and on course to work together for the good of the whole structure. There is nothing random. The further you lift yourself from the constraint of 'time' and 'reality' the more you will see how perfectly everything is being played out. In that place of timelessness where all is one and all is now, there is only perfection. If you can live with one foot in that place while keeping one foot on the floor, you will have mastered the secret of experiencing heaven on earth and earth in heaven.

Why do I feel pointless sometimes?

If you are feeling pointless that means the movement has already started. This is a big question – it is the beginning of the search, the one that starts the journey. When you are asking this question it means the answer is already available. It is already in your reality and on your path and your soul has access to the information. If you are asking this question you have already set up something profound so that you will find answers. Keep digging and you will find them. The Universe will always answer you. You will find your way. The true seeker will always find answers. Don't stop seeking and wondering, don't stop asking questions – and stay open to the answers because they may not be what you expect.

The real answer to this question is that you are everything all of the time and that cannot have a point because everything simply is. How can a rounded, full exquisite expression of divinity have or be a point? Yet feelings of pointlessness do happen, often when you feel as if you do not belong. Humans are tribal, communal beings and need community. In religious contexts people come together once a week on a designated day. People on a spiritual path often step away from that paradigm and think they can do the journey alone, but bodies need other bodies doing the same thing in order to feel part of something greater and to really get the truth. The body is the part of you that very quickly believes itself to be pointless until you find another body that holds the truth. Being part of a community helps your body to know that you belong.

Often what you are seeking when you feel pointless is to have a 'purpose', something to make you happy and fulfilled. By all means, go out and find what that is. Do whatever it takes to find the things that make your heart sing and then go out and do them, but do not confuse them with your 'purpose' or the 'point' of your existence. The truth is that your purpose is being lived every second. You are already on purpose. You don't have to change anything to be on purpose. Healers heal – they can't help themselves. They heal whether they are scrubbing a floor or leading a church group, working in a bank or running a healing practice, driving a bus or being a nurse. When you are the light, you are always the light, no matter what you choose to do with it. You are always on purpose. The more conscious you are, the more fun you can have with it, but you can never step out of your purpose. In the moments where you feel pointless or purposeless you have the opportunity to remember that your purpose in every moment is to step into your Divinity, into an enlightened understanding of life. The moments of pointlessness are just nudges to step back into the Allness. They are only there to remind you that your experiences of separateness are only ever experiences, not the truth.

How would it be if you could really integrate that into your knowingness? How would it be if you could really know that every breath is on purpose, that by being alive, you are living your purpose in this moment? How would it be if you could know that you are the point?

Why is there so much pain and suffering on Earth?

In a way, that's what you signed up for – an extraordinary game where you, as an individuated aspect of the One, went out into the world, to a planet where 'reality' contained judgement, separation, density and pain and suffering to see if, through the truly Divine and limitless light that you really are, you could guide that part of yourself home, back to the truth.

In this earthly reality, pain and suffering are calls to awakening. Have you ever noticed that when your life is going smoothly you don't learn a thing? You lie in the sun and you go with the stream and you evolve and develop not a jot. You don't learn who you are or what you are for or why you are here. It is only when you hit a bump that you start questioning and learning and looking at what you might need to change or modify in your life. The bumps in the road are the reasons you are a seeker. You know you are not truly here to suffer, so any time you find yourself struggling or suffering, you have another opportunity to get clearer of the conditioning and habits and thought patterns and old junk you have collected on your human journey. You get another chance to ask: What if there is another way?

If you can look at every bit of pain and suffering and discomfort as an opportunity to grow and heal and to learn exactly what your soul has requested to learn, you can begin to see it as something given to you by a loving Divine source for your highest good – for the highest good. You can begin to know that every moment has been precisely orchestrated so that you could have exactly the event you needed for the highest good. You can begin to trust that everything that happens is for the highest good – always. If you can really truly know this in the depths of your being you can let go of the judgements you hold about pain and suffering and the moment you let go of judgement, you no longer need to struggle. If you are honest with yourself, you will see that any experience of pain or suffering has the potential to lead you to immense knowledge and a capacity for compassion that you simply would not have had without the experience of 'suffering'.

The key is to keep coming back to this knowing. Often when you think you've got it you hit another judgement or you go into struggle and forget again. Part of your job is to continually remind yourself of what the truth really is – that although you may experience pain, suffering is optional. Pain is just a course corrector. It enables you to identify when you are off course and gives you an opportunity to change that. Suffering is what happens when you identify yourself with the pain, when you become the pain and think that it is the truth of who you are. Suffering is what happens when you judge the pain as wrong or bad. The moment you let go of the judgement you stop suffering.

The key is to begin to see every event as God's perfection unfolding. If you can really know that it is all Divine and all perfect then you no longer need to attract negativity into your reality – you no longer need to learn whatever it had to teach you. The more you see perfection, the more your life will reflect that. You attract what you judge because it gives you the opportunity to look at what you believe is not perfect and hear the voice of the Creator saying: "How is that not perfect? I only ever create perfection and I made that for you." When you are in judgement of a situation or person that situation or type of personality will be presented to you again and again until you can see it as God sees it and acknowledge the perfection of what it is. The quicker you learn to really get that 'this is perfect' the sooner you can let go of that situation from your reality – and then you don't ever have to experience it again. It really happens like that. If you truly have no judgement, if you can truly say this is perfect, you will never attract it into your reality again because it is no longer required to teach you anything. It is dealt with, it is done. Like everything that exists, you cannot ever fight it right. You can only love it right.

Why do terrible things happen?

Every single event is the outcome of a thought and a belief and a judgement. First look at the word 'terrible' which implies something that cannot be part of the Divine plan, otherwise why would it be termed terrible? That has never been the truth about any single thing that has ever happened in the history of time. It has all been perfectly, mathematically planned to help you move back towards the light and to help you move closer to your own Divine loving self. The Universe is astonishingly, mathematically precise, taking each small element to exactly the right place at exactly the right time for the experience your soul requested so that it could grow and evolve. Yes, you have choice and yes, you have free will, and you also live within the parameters of this perfect set-up.

Can you imagine the amount of organisation it takes to get the drunk driver to exactly the same corner as you at exactly the moment they drive into you? If you look back at that event you will find that the most amazing set of circumstances led to it and if you can be clear and not anxious or angry or in judgement about it, you can look at it with awe and see that you were taken to exactly where you needed to be to experience whatever it was you experienced. The lines of energy in every event are finer than a spider's web and the sacred geometry in those perfect lines of energy is astonishing.

The truth is that you are the Allness experiencing everything that exists and as the Allness, you first created 'terrible' events so that you could practice being in a state of total love. If you could be in a state of total love, nothing could touch you – not hate, nothing physical and in the end not even death so you tried it and it worked perfectly and you said: "That was easy. What if something really terrible happened?" and you tried that and it was again easy, so then you said: "This is too easy, let's pretend we are not the light and forget that we are love." So you did that and then 'terrible' really affected you. It was horrible.... And then you said, "Why me, God?" and you went into hate and judgement and felt completely victimised and had to revisit and revisit the whole process to get back to your original state of remembering that there is nothing so terrible that love cannot overcome it.

From a human perception this feels like a very dismissive answer of all the heavy 'real' situations in the world. Children starve, people are sold into slavery and the most awful abuses take place but not one of those events happened to someone who was not God in a body – whether they know it consciously or not. There is only one thing in the Universe and it is God, The Allness, The Absolute. Nothing else exists, so what you are looking at is Divine abusing Divine... which cannot happen unless there was an amazing soul contract entered into by each being which said: "No matter what it takes, I will help you heal."

You might ask: If all is Divine and all is perfect, why do we need to 'heal'? And what are we healing? Well, all is Divine and it is all perfect but unless you completely know that and feel it in your body, you still need healing. While you still believe that you are not that, you have to do everything you can to bring you to a state of no doubt. Ultimately that is why everyone is here and the biggest mission is just to walk each other home. When you do that you can look at your life and instead of judging it and yourself and everyone around you as harming and hurting you, you can thank each one for their part in walking you home.

When you have conversations with people who have been through tremendous crisis they will almost always say that they would not change what happened as that was when they really stepped up and realised that they were capable of so much more than they thought they were, that who they were was so much more than they realised. So was the terrible event terrible, or was it an amazing opportunity to become more than you ever knew you could be?

What about the really big stuff that happens on this planet when people die in tsunamis, there is mass genocide, whole nations go through ethnic cleansing? What is the bigger picture there?

When you start asking questions like this you have already had the nudge that ultimately brings you to enlightenment. You are being given another magnificent opportunity to look beyond what you see in 3D. Every single being on this planet has come here with the opportunity to become enlightened. That includes the ones for whom it looks as if there will never be an opportunity to wake up and it includes those who are deemed so 'evil' that they clearly are never going to be enlightened like all the lovely light workers... These are often the ones who came back to be of great service as they had already achieved enlightenment and they realised that so many were so stuck in the sensory experience of this planet that without something to get them to start the journey they would stay stuck. So the big guns like Hitler came, along with the ordinary drunk driver or drug pusher or war-monger or pro-Sharia Imam. Every one of them came here on a contract that said: "No matter what it takes, I will help you heal".

On a human level these huge scale events can seem overwhelmingly dreadful when you see something happening to large groups of people. When you separate it out into each soul's journey, each soul having an experience for their highest good, it feels more manageable. Nothing is an accident. Each 'victim' made the soul decision based on whatever it was their soul requested for them to experience and to learn and to heal and to reach their highest potential. Every single event, however terrible it looked, was an opportunity to heal, to step back into the light and in that process, give this planet an extra piece of information even if that information is just to show humanity that they no longer need to do it this way. Group contracts are made for the good of the whole. A group decides that they are going to have a collective experience so that the population never has to learn that lesson again. Everyone in the group commits to having an experience so that everyone else can remember how not to do life in future.

The Dalai Lama once met an old Tibetan monk who had been imprisoned in Tibet. When he asked the monk if he had ever felt in danger for his life in jail his response was that the greatest risk he experienced was that of losing compassion for his jailers. What if every terrible thing that happened on the planet is an opportunity for humanity to remember compassion? Compassion for those who are suffering, compassion for those who create the suffering, compassion for the human condition. Compassion, unconditional love and unconditional acceptance take you right out of victim mode and into the heart. From a place of unconditional love and acceptance of what is, what could be labelled terrible? If a child dies, that is a shock for the physical body. For the powerful being of light who finished his job? No shock. He did exactly what he set out to do. What if every step along your journey is actually Christ's journey? He knew that if you are in love, nothing can touch you and the way you get to that state is by constantly choosing unconditional love, in every situation, in every circumstance.

These big global happenings are often massive wake-up calls. Communities come together, people open their hearts and their homes. There is always, always a higher picture and even if you don't know what it is, if you can trust in that, you stay out of judgement, blame and fear and you move even deeper into love and when you do that, you begin to change the make-up of the planet and its people. When you reside in love, that is what you create. When you reside in anger and judgement and grief and sadness that is what you create. These mass events are always times of huge potential shift on the planet to give everyone another opportunity to move into love rather than stay in fear.

Why is there so much fear on this planet?

A huge part of the human journey is to get beyond fear because fear is based on judgement and judgement attracts to you the thing you judge and the thing you fear, setting up a downward spiral that perpetuates the fear in each individual and on the planet. The chaotic reality being created continuously on this planet has a lot to do with the basic misunderstanding of fear. If you are Divine how can you be in fear? Fear and Divine are mutually exclusive, they cannot sit in the same place because the moment you step into fear you say there is no God. If that is your stance that is a whole different story and you have many lifetimes to play with that idea. If you are on a conscious path of enlightenment the moment you step into fear you disconnect from your Divine self because your Divine self knows that all is perfect and is working exactly as it should.

If someone walks around the corner right this minute with a gun and points it at your head, your Divine self says, ok, my time is up. Your fearful self says it is all wrong and shouldn't be happening. This is a complete misunderstanding. If it shouldn't happen it won't happen. If your time is your time the gun will go off whether someone pulls the trigger or not. It is all set up and it is all perfect and the minute you step into fear you have stepped into confusion, you have stepped into judgement, you have stepped out of your truth. Your body holds the memory of death in its cells and it knows that it could die but your soul knows you can never die, that death is not the truth. Your choice now is to live more and more from truth, from the soul's knowing and the more you do that the more you step out of fear and into a place where you see the perfection of all things.

How would it be if instead of getting scared or angry about the things you see on the news every night and the state of the planet you honoured the journey of each being who is creating their own perfect reality in order to learn and grow and heal and remember that they are Divine? How would it be if you just really held a space for each person's story you hear, honouring their choices, acknowledging the depth of their commitment to helping you heal by having that experience? How would it be if instead of judging any of it you could honour their existence and their choice? How would that sit next to fear? Wouldn't that clear it a little bit?

You see, life is an illusion. It was all meant to be fun but you decided to take it seriously so you could get the most out of it. Wherever you placed your focus, wherever you decided you would get the biggest lesson and the most benefit, this is where you decided to go again and again. At Disney World there are rides that are meant to be fun but in fact they are very scary. Disney World is where you now live and you can choose to go into the Tunnel of Love or the places where there are ghosts and monsters. You are now at such a clear point in your journey that you can decide to take the scary ride one more time to see if there is anything in you that still believes in the illusion or you can cash in your tickets, pack your bags and go home. It is all illusion and it is all choice. Just be very clear on where you are. Do you want to play the game to the full in Disney World or do you want to step out of the illusion? You can even decide that you want to work there and add to the fearfulness of the rides for the little new ones coming up behind you. Then you can get very serious about all the terrors on the planet and all the bad things that are happening and you can make speeches about it to everyone around you and you can help to make it more real for them so that they can also feel the fear. It is entirely up to you how you want to play it. None of it is real. Every moment of your life you can choose how you want to feel.

Decide if fear is still serving you. Does it help you to feel more like a Divine being having a human experience? Is it there to help you stay in touch with your heart and is it growing your compassion? If that is the case then use it and let it serve you. If that is not the case then look again and do whatever it takes to get your soul's vote into your body. Fear is a purely physical thing. Your soul has no understanding of the concept. It knows itself to be eternal and Divine and it knows it has existed through all of time without being damaged or killed or being anything other than pure loving light. All the rest of your emotional responses come from your physical self. All of life is just an opportunity to experience. In this moment you can choose. Do you want to feel more fear or do you want to breathe in your truth?

The light is in the air around you. Breathe into your solar plexus, imagining a bright golden light beginning to grow in the centre of your being. Add the words "I Am" and feel that light expanding. Keep breathing consciously, each breath bringing more of your soul into your body and then know the truth about yourself: "I Am. I Am ancient powerful being of light. I have never been damaged through all of existence." Just feel that light expanding. If you keep doing this you will find that there is a recognition in your cells of the truth of what you really are and one morning you will wake up and the fear will be less and soon it will hardly be there at all. Fear is not there to teach you how to handle fear better, it is there to teach you courage. It is there to teach you how to stop pretending to be only human, less than perfect and far away from the Divine. It is there to guide you back to the Allness and your own Divine soul self. Thank it for its gift then step into your soul self where fear does not exist and let your body get the truth.

Why do so many people suffer from depression and what can we do when we experience it?

Depression is a paradox. It is a deep level of spiritual confusion but it actually holds the potential for enlightenment. It is a life choice in the sense that all life is choice. If this is what you choose to experience it is so that you can get to a place beyond judgement of God. If you look at the world in its current state it appears deeply insane, inhumane, chaotic and on the constant brink of war, famine and disaster so on the surface, depression might seem the only response of a sane human. How could you not be depressed?

From an enlightened position, the world is the place where every soul which wants to grow and develop comes for the lessons it needs. From this space, if you look clearly you will see that the Divine functions according to perfect and mathematically precise rules of cause and effect. Depression is merely an opportunity to look again at what seems like madness and stop judging it on all levels. It offers the opportunity to look again without needing things to be a certain way. What if even a brain chemical imbalance that causes suicidal depression is a choice that the soul made to get beyond its need to run the Universe and to tell it how it is meant to look and function? As everything is ultimately an opportunity to learn, even suicide is not the end of anything. It is often just another opportunity – this time for everyone around the suicide to learn to let go of guilt and judgement. There really is nothing wrong in the Universe. There are just many, many opportunities to heal and learn and grow. Everything in your school curriculum was there to teach you something whether it was a subject you loved or hated. At the very least it taught you how to think and if you look at the big picture everything that has happened in your life has brought you to who you are now with the information and understanding you now have.

This is a short answer to an enormously complex problem and if you are suffering from depression, it is not going to help you to know that you are just in the process of living and learning – except that it is the truth of the situation. It is one of the many way-showers that you put along your path to make sure you would stay on it. That is the soul's truth and if you have difficulty even believing that you have a soul then this answer is going to make no sense at all but if you know there is the possibility that you have a soul then you are already half way to a cure. Psychology is ultimately the study of the soul, although the use of the Greek term 'psyche' removes conscious acknowledgement of that. When the soul is included in your awareness everything else will work as well and depression will be seen as something that is just there to get you to focus on your soul again. Depression is a soul imbalance, in the sense that if you become out of touch with your soul it manifests as depression and every other malaise that humans suffer from.

Nothing was meant to be so hard. Every difficulty humans suffer with and from was created simply to bring you back to your centre, to bring you back to your soul. The moment you bring your focus back to your soul and you allow yourself to hear your soul's truth and feel the expansion that it brings, you will know that there is only one truth: You are a magnificent expression of Divine love and nothing else exists. It is only when you temporarily forget this that the world explodes or implodes around you. Not one of those actively involved in making wars or creating chaos woke up this morning and acknowledged their souls. They are running on fear and anger which is the opposite of the soul's truth. Reconnect with your soul. Reconnect with the love inside you that is who you truly are. Keep breathing in your I Amness. Ask your Higher Self to show you the underlying feelings and find whatever techniques or tools serve you best to release them. And remember to look up – quite literally.

Isn't there more to life than just this?

The short answer: Yes, there is! This question comes from such a teenage stance, a feeling that life owes you – you've got your driver's licence and you're earning money and you thought it was going to be such fun but you're just getting up, going to work, coming home, going to bed and it feels like a tiny, boring existence – but it is often the beginning of the spiritual search. When you are in this place it is an opportunity to step into acceptance and peace with yourself and your life. From there you can start to become aware and listen to that voice within telling you there is so much more. All you have to do is look. All you have to do is open your eyes. Open your awareness and your sensitivity to the widest degree. Step into your awareness of the Divine functioning in each moment, then you can be of service and when you are of service you will feel as if you are on purpose. The moment you are on purpose your service has value because your service is not from a place of: "I'm powerful and you're weak", your service is: "I Am Divine and I see that in you." If you can see the Divine in another they will reflect back the Divine in you and suddenly your question becomes irrelevant. In the Allness of everything that is, in that place where only the Allness exists and you are part of it, you can see that this is all there is but it is ALL there is.

Why do some people have so much and others have so little?

You have exactly what you believe you deserve and you have exactly what your soul came to experience. Some beings came to play with extreme wealth to see what they could learn and experience from playing the game of life on the rich side. Others are starving in a desert to learn about that experience and to add to the information of the Allness. There truly is not just one version of you on the planet so while one part of you is playing the prince, another is playing the pauper. The Higher Self, like the motherboard, is collating all the information from all these incarnations and aspects of beingness and adding it to the matrix and the knowledge that will then become available to all.

The picture is so big and so complex that it really does not help to try and make sense of it from a single tiny perspective. Focus instead on what is happening in the little speck of reality that you are currently inhabiting and make that the biggest shiniest thing you possibly can. That is all you are asked to do, to create a reality that is abundantly light and joyous and polish your life until it shines. The more loving, compassionate, abundant and joyous your life is the more you add to the greatness of the Allness, but as the Allness is All, if you are starving and suffering, your job is simply to do that to the deepest degree so that the Allness can totally have the experience of lack and limitation and disease and horror. It really is just a huge experiment that everyone signed up for and the more you see it as that and the more you 'play' your role the quicker the experiment will be completed and you can sign up for a new exciting game in another galaxy.

Why is communication so difficult?

In the story of the Tower of Babel, humans got together to build a tower all the way up to heaven to try and get back to their heavenly state. Building a tower was clearly not the way to get to heaven because the whole aim of the exercise of being human was for each one to find the connection with their Divine selves so God made them all speak different languages and from that point on no one could really communicate with anyone else. Communication is essentially something completely artificial that was created when you lost your sense of connection to the Divine and forgot that everything is part of the One. Now you have the internet and the media and the most amazing ways to instantly communicate but essentially everyone still speaks and listens in their own language so no matter what you say the other person is always going to hear through the filter of every experience they have ever had.

In a sense any difficulty you have with communication is a soul construct to try and get you back to your natural state where you actually really listen to what the other person is saying without filtering any of it – soul to soul. That is the only way you will make sense out of anything. Look at what happens to the energy field of someone who says that the worst thing anyone can do is lie to them. They are already in so much judgement that they will absolutely not recognise the truth if it flies out and bites them in the face. Tune in and listen to the energy of what each person says and you will be much closer to what they are really trying to communicate and what you will find is that what everyone is really communicating is, "Please find a way to love me." That is the only thing anyone ever says, whichever words they are using. Listen to the energy instead of the words and you will hear the truth all the time. Train yourself to listen to the energy and you will hear that all communication is a need to be recognised, accepted and loved. No one ever really says anything else.

Release the memories of persecution that happened in the past when you communicated something that seemed important to you, and once the judgement and the energy around it is gone, communication will not seem difficult any more. Communication becomes the thing you be and do in a world where everything is about communication because everything is about energy. Communication is not difficult. Communicate what needs to happen in the moment. Let go of fear, let go of judgement. Connect with your feelings and communicate with your energy and it becomes the easiest thing there is.

Why is there so much misunderstanding in our communications?

Misunderstanding is a game you play, it is not the truth. Misunderstanding says you are outside of your Divine self and you are playing a small human game. Misunderstanding says you choose not to hear the other person – and why would you create that energy in your life? Look at that pattern, look at what you believe about yourself, look at how you believe people will treat you, look at your judgements, look at what you have experienced and what you have locked into place in your reality.

Step into your Divine self and there can be no misunderstanding. Souls do not misunderstand one another, souls do not misunderstand anything. Souls have access to the truth. If you are misunderstanding it is because you are manipulating something. If you are in tune there is no misunderstanding. There is no real misunderstanding on this planet. The minute you are in tune you can hear what goes on underneath the words. The minute you listen with your heart there is no room for misunderstanding. The truth is you are listening with so much of yourself. You pretend to do it with ten percent of your brain but in truth you listen with your body, with your energy field, you listen with your soul, you listen on so many levels and if you are conscious and clear on how you are listening to somebody you will absolutely know the truth of what they are saying.

What can we learn from our children?

Everything! Your children are not your children. They are powerful beings of light who chose you to incarnate through and they have come mainly to teach. You have signed up as their students and they have graciously agreed to come and be your teachers. Every generation has come in to develop the species a step further up the ladder of evolution and their parents are the lucky ones to be first in line for what they have to teach. Be endlessly grateful for the gift they have brought to you as their parents.

Really let the truth of that sink into your cells and then know that every moment you have judged yourself for what you believe you have done to damage your children was basically a misunderstanding. Your maths teacher was not damaged by your mistake, just as your children were not damaged by what was essentially the way you got to develop your soul-self. Now take another step back and remember that you were your parents' teacher. They did not in any way, shape or form damage you. They were there as your students and they learnt precisely what they needed from you. The hierarchy of the soul truth is never what you expect it to be. The powerful being that you are came to teach your parents the deepest lessons that they ever learnt in their lifetime, just as you are being taught by your children. Sit with that for a bit and feel where you resist that thought. It might even be good practice to have a discussion with your parents in a meditation and let them feel to you how true that is and how much they appreciate your teaching and the gifts your soul has given them. Remember there are not young and old souls – there is just one soul of which everyone is an aspect and as such you choose how you need to experience life and why. You also choose teachers and students and as so often in the physical 'real' world, it is actually the reverse of what you think it will be. The ones you think you are teaching are so often your teachers.

Your children are the ones you set up to take you to the next level. Most of the children coming in now to the planet have come from the future. They have come to show you how Ascension can happen in a physical body. Your body knows that there is a light but up to this point you have had to drop the body to get there so the body in its animal form believes that life is good and death is bad. Ascension looks like a death process, so the body says: "No thank you, I will not join this time around." Your soul does not need to ascend, it is already the light and it knows this, but as aspects of the Divine living out an experience of being physical, you are seeking now to take the body with you into the light, to remove every bit of negative belief about the body, to begin to see it as an aspect of the Divine, as congealed light, as light made manifest in a solid form. If you could absolutely know that, you could live in the enlightened state without having to drop the body and come back to do over. It will happen in this lifetime, the bodies will shift into the light as they are reminded of what they really are and your children absolutely know this and have come to help you remember. The children who are coming in now have already been through that process and their gift to you is to come back in bodies that remember, because bodies communicate with each other. These children have been through the Ascension process and they will come and hold a space for your body so that instead of going into fear you will understand that it is doable.

It was not a particularly easy or fun journey for these children to come back to the past. At the time it seemed a great idea but from their shiny, light perspective, coming back to a reality where the beings still think they are so separate that they can kill each other – that's a shock! What they see are beings who still don't know that they and the planet are the same thing. That's a shock. They see beings who are mercilessly taking from the planet without putting anything back. That's a shock. The whole idea of separation is a huge shock and they have had to make friends with all of it and remember that they are here to show you that there is another way. They are here to step you into your truth of being Divine, being light and living that. They are here to show you that it is possible to live as one, not in separation. That is what your children can teach you and it is the most profound gift.

What about children with learning difficulties, ADHD, Aspergers, Autism... all the things that make it so difficult for them to be here? What is the truth about them?

There is not one soul who arrives on the planet exactly the same as anyone else or who fits perfectly into what might be labelled 'normal' so the question is simply how do you deal with everyone and what do they have to teach you? Conditions such as ADHD and Aspergers are not new, they were just not known and named in previous times. Through the media more people are now aware of every human condition and that is why everything suddenly looks as if it has reached epidemic proportions. In addition, the old way of bringing up children to be seen and not heard and the biblical injunction not to spare the rod, meant that in past times no one knew that a child's personality was this or that. No one was interested in them in any way other than to control them or make use of them. In many societies children are still given work as soon as they can walk and no one worries about whether they are calmly 'normal' or hyper ADD so this is essentially a first world situation.

These children have come to show everyone on the planet that the time has come for change. As the planet shifts from a third dimensional state to a fifth dimensional state the old ways of doing things no longer work. The sins of the fathers can no longer be visited on the children. Time has run out and all these issues are coming up so that they can be brought to awareness, so that unfinished business can be completed. Every single judgement is now being highlighted so that you can move beyond it. You are being asked to acknowledge that the Universe is perfectly run, so take a look at what is keeping you from seeing that. What is your judgement that is the one thing you cannot move beyond? Is it the pain your less-than-perfect child is suffering? Is that what stops you from living in heaven on earth? So then have a whole family of autistic/Aspergers/ADHD boys in your family and begin to find a way to see the perfection in that situation and let go of needing to control the perfection of the Universe.

These beings, these children with all these conditions, what about them? What do they get out of giving you the opportunity to let go of your judgement? These 'different' children are souls who have come to be of the greatest sacrificial service the planet has ever seen. The truth is that they are almost a different species as their gifts are such a rare thing on a planet that is on the brink of wiping itself out through greed and self-destructive hatred. These children are incapable of judgement and their gift is to help humanity move beyond it. Their gift is profound. Their experience is not particularly easy and even though it often looks as if they are out of touch with emotions, they have come to keep their parents, peers and teachers very much in touch with their emotions. If you move beyond the facade they show, there is an almost impossible amount of heart energy pumping through them. They are specifically endowed with this heart energy as they do not filter it through the normal human experience of feelings. Because part of their emotional body is switched off they hold much more of the true energy of unconditional love. Remember, that is not the case for 'normal' humans. Humans are wired to judge and place conditions, so for the energy of unconditional love to be poured into the matrix of the planet, it took a large number of beings to incarnate who could hold that energy without burning out. These children came to hold that unconditional love with their energy bodies.

They have come from the future and other dimensions and their whole journey is to help shift the consciousness on the planet. They are enlightened souls who did not come to learn or balance anything for themselves. They came purely to be of service and to help the planet move forward into the fifth dimension because their bodies have already been through that event, that shift, and they are here in bodies that are communicating that to all the other bodies that have gone into fear and resistance. Their souls are doing this while their bodies are pretending to be your children so that you can let go of your judgement and relax into the knowledge that there is an outcome that will shift the whole planet to the next level.

There seems to be so much abuse and cruelty towards animals on this planet. What role do they play and how can we help them?

Everything on this planet and every other planet for that matter and everywhere in between is part of the Allness, the Absolute, God/Goddess, All that is. Of course animals are part of that and as part of that they are doing exactly what you are on the planet – they are having an experience and adding to the knowledge the Allness has of itself. They are all on track exactly as you are. They are having exactly the experience their souls need for their highest good.

Part of why they have the experiences they do is so that you can look at non-judgement and unconditionality from every angle. Rather than using your energy to hate the people who are abusive or cruel, the greatest thing you can do to support the animals on their journey is hold as much love as you are capable of at all times. In many ways animals are much closer to the angels than humans. They are endlessly forgiving. They judge nothing, they remain able to love under extreme circumstances and they are never vengeful or unforgiving. They are always prepared to give humans another chance. So love them and learn from them and remember to not judge any of what is going on. Animals give you an extreme opportunity to practice non-judgement and they are so very, very good at helping you step into compassion. They have come to hold a space for you to learn to honour their choices and to remember to be extremely grateful for their endless gifts and endless sacrifice for the highest good.

How can we stop people from turning against one another?

Who are you and who am I and what on earth are we? If I am Divine and you are Divine then what part of the Divine can turn against another part of the Divine? How would that work? It would be like your foot deciding to start a war against your hand. It sounds insane and yet that is what is happening everywhere on the planet. While humanity continues to live the lie of separation, each person is always going to be warring with another part of themselves and what you are asked to do from every level is to get back to loving your neighbour. Love your neighbour as yourself and know your neighbour as yourself. There is no separation, so there is no neighbour and there is no self. There is no one to turn against and when even one person can get that, really get it, the whole world will change.

When you finally understand that all is one and that turning against another is just a misunderstanding of everything that is, you can begin to return to the truth. You can begin to remember that if there is nothing outside of you, nothing bad can happen to any aspect of you. If you can deeply and truly remember who you are and what you are and what everyone is, you can get back to your true state. That is the point of the whole journey. There is only one. There has never been anything else. Turning against one another is as mad as biting your toe. Take another look and insist on seeing the big picture. Look at the truth and keep the vision of the truth always in front of you and do not let anything interfere with it. That is why you exist and that is your mission and your role – to be that and to teach it. Everything else is extraneous.

What happens when we die?

Your body is dense and heavy in vibration as it carries not just the memories of all you have been since time began, but also the emotional impact of those memories. No wonder you feel so heavy so often. When you release all of that in the moment of death you have already started experiencing the light of bliss that exists on the other side. By the time the car crashes or the bullet hits, your soul is outside and watching the body doing whatever it is doing, which is often just whatever the people around you need to be able to fully let you go. Your soul returns to its natural state which is love. You immediately lose all the heaviness and grief and confusion and you are back in your true soul state where all the truth exists, but without the weight of the emotions and in particular the weight of the judgements that you carry in your body.

Death is the highlight of life. Comparatively speaking, birth is often a very painful and difficult event whereas death is truly the easiest thing anyone will ever experience. It is a joyful happy celebration that always comes at exactly the right moment. For your soul it is the whole point of your life. It says that everything you needed to do in this life is finally done and it is now time to go home and claim the prize. There is a sudden expansion into the light and truth where all information is suddenly clear and available. It is expansive and joyous and completely painless. Do not ever get involved in horror stories about death. There is never a soul that hangs around wondering if it was loved. When you hear of spirits that are 'stuck', that is someone who got a small part of themselves hooked into a judgement and had to learn to release that before they could gather all their aspects together again.

The moment the body is dropped the soul is completely back to its natural state which is only love and you have moved away from any sense of separation. Separation only seems real when you are living in a body because it has a clear boundary of skin that separates it from all other bodies. Souls do not have any sense of loss or separation. Your soul knows that everyone you have ever loved is always with you. When you die every single being you have ever loved meets you on the other side. Not just the ones who have died before you but your children and your friends and everyone you have loved are all there in their light bodies welcoming you home and honouring your experience of life and what you have learnt and achieved. You are so multi-levelled that the piece of the soul that does all the work down here in the physical is just a small part of your vastness and there is definitely a part of you that is always ready for the party to welcome a soul back to its true state.

You are so magical. You are so magnificent. You are the most exciting creation! The journey forward is to return your body to its true state where all judgement is gone and where it will blend with your soul again and you will not have to drop it to experience constant bliss.

Have we all had past lives?

This is basically a question of faith. There is no real proof except that people can be hypnotised into 'remembering' past lives but of course the soul truth is that energy keeps on going whether it is focused through a particular physical body or not. So yes, everyone who is alive has been alive before and will keep on being alive for ever more. There will be different experiences and expressions of being alive but life is certainly ongoing. If time is not what you think it is and if souls are essentially all one then it becomes very difficult to try and make logical sense out of past and future lifetimes and as it is all an illusion anyway – a dream, really – so it becomes very difficult to explain non-third dimensional reality in a way that makes sense in the third dimension.

If you can imagine a very big, very bright light above the planet that sends down many, many rays of light and each of those rays is an expression of a separate human then you can begin to see how it works. Each of those rays is part of the big light but they are also separate energies which have lowered the vibration of the light into a dense third dimensional body. The body lives and dies but the light remains part of the big light and wherever that ray of light lands, whether it is the past or the future or this dimension or planet or some other dimension or planet it always remains part of the One. This is a very simplistic explanation of a very complex issue and a very advanced mathematician might be able to explain it all mathematically so that you would see how profoundly and precisely the whole system works, but you get the idea.

Everyone has had lives in the past and will continue to have them. You have had them on this planet and in this dimension and many other planets and dimensions but you have never not been part of the One. You are it and it is you and that is how it has always been and always will be. It does not work that a being like Cleopatra dies and then comes back as Queen Elizabeth I who then comes back as a baker in a village in Germany and then as a starving baby in Ethiopia. The piece of the light that had the lifetime as Cleopatra dies and goes back to the light and now that experience is part of the light and any part of the light can take that piece of experience and use that for the life that they then choose to live. Millions of pieces of light can take a bit of that memory so there is not one strand that comes back and back, rather all strands become one and then come back as another aspect of the light with information to use to ultimately bring knowledge and experience to the light. Every time any one being does that, the light, God, the Allness expands and knows more of itself.

What is karma?

Since the time of Christ karma has no longer existed. His whole teaching was that you were in a state of grace and therefore beyond karma. There was no longer a need for retribution or an eye for an eye. Karma was constructed so that you could keep track of things but it was never about retribution. It was always about balancing. You are not punished for touching a live wire by being shocked. You are simply experiencing cause and effect. Reality has no emotional involvement. Karma is the same. If you hold your hand over the flame your hand will burn. It is the nature of your hand and the nature of the flame. If you hurt someone reality will create balance and you will get to experience the same feeling and it will feel ten times worse because even if you can imagine someone else's pain, you cannot really experience it. You only experience your own pain in real terms.

So what happens when you become conscious? You step into a totally different reality. You begin to take responsibility for every action and every event and the more you do that the more you step into grace. The moment you begin to remember who you are, you no longer play out the old game in the old way. When you are utterly conscious of what you do and you have no judgement on any of it – not what you do nor what is done to you – at that moment you step into grace and the whole concept of karma disappears. When you are love, there is no judgement. When you are love there is no pain, so suddenly the idea of hurting or getting hurt becomes redundant. If you are love, you are Divine and the Divine owes nothing to the Divine. The Divine cannot hurt the Divine so although there is a perfect book-keeping system, it is all paid and clear when you step back into love – and that takes you right out of consensus reality. If you are in a state of perfect love, you can go and sit in a fire and it will not touch you. You can get yourself nailed to a cross and you will not be killed. That is the whole point of the teaching. There is book-keeping and there is love. Love trumps all the rest.

How can we be truly free?

Freedom is a huge thing in human consciousness, in fact this might be the biggest question of all. It is certainly the first one you have to deal with when you are born. The first overwhelming feeling in the moment when your huge, powerful soul settles into a tiny, helpless human body is one of loss of freedom. Suddenly your soul is contained and bound in every way and all its freedom appears to be gone. The whole experience of being in a body is the opposite of freedom. If you do not breathe, drink and eat your body will expire and you can use that to feel bound every moment. There are endless rules that society forces upon you that restrict who you are allowed to be and what you are allowed to do and then there is religion just to make things even more interesting. The state of being human appears to be the state of being not free – but that is the greatest illusion of all.

The biggest lesson you have to learn is that you are a free soul, not a bound human. You are a free soul in a human body. This is a very important step which is why it is coming up in global consciousness in such a big way at the moment. Some nations and religions are threatening to remove it altogether while others run things in ways that pretend to keep everyone safe but which do not create freedom of any kind. When something suddenly pops up everywhere it is definitely an opportunity for everyone to look again at what it is and what it means.

You attract what you judge and as lack of freedom is one of your biggest judgements so you have had to experience it in every way possible. Your feeling of lack of freedom and your judgement on the bondage you believe you are in creates absolutely every expression of lack of freedom, from jails to slavery to bodies that are not able to function normally. You have fought for freedom through the ages and you have been persecuted for what you believed, said and did. You have been enslaved in all sorts of ways and the more conscious you became, the more you were aware of how little freedom you were being given. The only way to get back to your true state is to entirely remember the truth: You are a free powerful soul experiencing everything that the Divine is and when you fully remember that, you are not only completely free but you are on your way to an ascended state of enlightenment.

How can you not be free? Soul is soul, Divine is Divine, free is free. There isn't anything other. If you are in your truth you are completely, utterly, absolutely free. Your freedom is within you and it has nothing to do with your outer reality. If freedom is your natural state it is obviously a misunderstanding to expect someone to give it to you. You are either free or you are not. Freedom is the state of being in your truth and you either are that or you are not. You are either in your truth – in which case you are free – or you are not in your truth in which you won't feel free, but you are still free. When you are being God you can do that in a jail cell and you are free no matter what the outside truth appears to be. If you are being God you are free. If you are playing God and you want to control everything you are totally in bondage to your misunderstanding.

Freedom is a very advanced spiritual state and you have to know that and be it – not fight for it outside yourself. When everyone truly understands that, all will instantly be free. You now have to take freedom seriously as the next step along your spiritual path. Every breath and every thought has to bring you back to truth. You are free in your deepest inner being where only truth beyond any of the illusion exists.

The Personal Questions: All About 'Me'

Why don't I ever feel good enough?

There are many voices in your head and the loudest is the one that tells you that you are not good enough. If you can actively disengage from it and step back into your true voice, your deepest, inner voice, the still, small voice within, that voice will never tell you that you are not good enough. That voice knows your essence, knows that you are Divine, knows who you really are. For some reason you are wired to hear the noise rather than the quiet.

Go into the quiet and there you will find the truth, the unbelievable magnificence of you. In each moment when you are feeling not enough, switch off the noise and step into the quiet for a second. That's all it will take – literally just disengage for a second from the noisy nonsense in your head and step back into the quiet space of Divine truth and you'll so clearly hear how good enough you are and that you are Divine. How can you not be Divine? How can you not be good enough when you are Divine? How can you not step into the truth of that? The more you do it the easier it will become. Have this as part of your practice. Remind yourself of the truth. It really is a discipline to quiet the other noisy voices and know that in the quiet you will hear the truth, the Divine voice, the Divine truth.

What can I do to not feel so guilty?

Look at guilt very clearly. Look it squarely in the eye. Guilt is the biggest misunderstanding on the planet because it implies that something is wrong. You most likely feel guilty because you believe you did something wrong. The question is, how could that have happened in this perfect Universe where things are run with mathematical precision? How did you manage to step out of the plan and do something wrong? When were you bigger than God? There is a perfect plan and you cannot screw it up.

Now, look at your judgement on God and where you hold that God messed things up. The only way you, as an aspect of the Divine, can judge yourself as guilty is if you judge God as guilty. If God is a perfect being that can, because of its nature, create only perfection, you as an aspect of God can therefore not have done anything wrong. There never has been a mistake in all of creation. There never will be any mistakes in all of creation – so guilt is based on an impossibility.

The next level of this question relates to why you feel guilty. Every healer on the planet came in with a huge chunk of guilt and that is a very specific part of the journey. In the language of colour, guilt and healing are both magenta. Magenta is the colour above the crown where the red which relates to everything physical is combined with the violet of everything spiritual and a healer needs that balance of spirit and matter. Healers need to put their spirituality on the ground in the physical world to be able to make any kind of difference. Now, what are you trying to make a difference to? Everyone else's pain. And why do they have pain? They have pain because pain is a by-product of guilt. Every bit of struggle or pain is a guilt feeling that is looking for punishment.

Your biggest job as a healer is to help everyone who comes to you to understand that guilt is not real and you can only do that if you have learnt the lesson yourself and managed to let go of your own guilt feelings, so look at it logically and remember your own Divine nature and the nature of the Divine which is perfect. Do a process to connect with the memory of what it is you have carried through lifetime after lifetime that you have been too scared to look at because it was so awful. Trust your Higher Self to show you what you believe you did that was so unspeakable that you have had to feel so guilty. Now, go a step further and look through the eyes of your Higher Self at the people you thought you hurt, those poor victims who could not defend themselves against your evil doings. Really look and feel. Were they victims or were they powerful beings of light who came to you because you were the one who was strong enough and loved them enough to allow them to have the experience that they needed for their growth and highest good? Truth… Let your body get the truth. Were you guilty or were you the one who allowed something that they signed up for to happen?

The bottom line is that there is no such thing as guilt. You never got it wrong. You are Divine, you are experiencing being a perfectly on-track Divine human. There isn't a God who judges you. How can love judge? Where is guilt in love? Where is judgement in love? There is only love. If there is any part of you that can resonate with that, put down the guilt. Give it up. If you look through the eyes of guilt you will see only guilt. If you look through the eyes of love you will see only love.

How do I truly and deeply forgive myself?

This can be a lifetime's work or it can happen in a heartbeat. It can be such a difficult one – or the easiest thing to do. Either way, it needs a quantum shift in consciousness. It needs you to really look at reality differently. The only reason you could want to not forgive yourself is that it is too seductive not to forgive someone else. Who are you finding it so difficult to forgive that you need to keep punishing yourself rather than let someone else revert to innocence?

Take a look at your life and go back to the worst thing that ever happened to you. Look very honestly at who you were before that event then look at who you are now and begin to admit that you grew and developed more through that event than through any time of ease and happiness. So was the event bad or was it the most helpful thing that ever happened? With that understanding is it possible for you now to forgive the perpetrator and take the extra step of beginning to extend gratitude to the person or people who created the grief? Even if it is a struggle, if you just start to think the words "thank you great teacher" every time they cross your mind you will begin to shift the energy and eventually you will think of them with only genuine gratitude and you will have taken another great leap forward in your journey.

The next step is to look at the terrible thing that you did for which you can never be forgiven. What if that was the most difficult thing you were asked to do and you said yes because you were big enough and able to love enough to actually create that level of growth for another person? Please take this very seriously. Even if the other person died because of something you did, please remember who you are dealing with. There are only powerful beings of light experiencing all the facets of being human and the rest is simply the play. Death is not real. If there was a soul who left the planet because of something you did, feel for that soul and ask them what happened. They will always tell you that there has never been even one mistake since the Universe was created and that it was their perfectly chosen time to go. You did not manage to screw up God's plan. If it was someone who caused the death of someone you love and you are not able to forgive them, please talk to the soul of your loved one and you will always, always find that their soul feels only gratitude for the person who helped them off the planet. Do not believe anyone who tells you that there are angry souls wandering around seeking vengeance against murderers. Those are simply little entities that got stuck in the story and because they like the negative energy they hang around to try and create more negativity.

The truth about forgiving or not forgiving yourself is to see truth or to live a lie. When you cannot let go of your mistakes in the past you are essentially seeing yourself as outside of the truth that there is a Divine Power and that there is a plan and that the plan is working with mathematical precision. That is the truth, however if you are insisting on claiming that you are not able to be forgiven, you are claiming that you are the only piece of creation that is outside of the plan and either you are bigger than God and you managed to screw up the plan or there is no plan. Obviously if you really believe there is no plan, you still have many lifetimes to work out this issue and you should stop reading now. If, however, you can get your head around the idea of a Divine being that has a perfect plan then it just becomes a form of insanity to insist that you are guilty. Where is the logic in that?

The absolute soul truth is that there a perfect plan that works exactly as it is meant to and the more you commit to that truth the more you get to see the big picture and the more you get to connect to the life you wish to have. The more you get to experience that life the more you connect to joy and then you begin to create heaven on earth – and that is what you really came to do.

What do I do when I can't get past my anger?

Take a look at who you are angry with. You see, nothing is real, everything is a mirror. The anger is always an experience of yourself, it is a reflection of what you feel about yourself. For everyone, except perhaps a few enlightened souls, anger is a real experience of being on the planet. Most humans somewhere along the line have an extreme sense of frustration and anger about their lives and it is a wholly human emotion. Your soul is incapable of being angry. Anger is nothing other than fear masquerading as something else. Under its guise you can pretend to be stronger and bigger and more puffed up than you actually are so that you can fight or frighten off whatever is scaring you. It is not real. It is the cat's fur standing on end so that it looks bigger to the dog. The problem is that once you have unleashed your anger and managed to scare someone into some kind of submission it becomes very addictive because it creates such a lovely buzz of false power. If you can strut around with your armour rattling and your weapons at the ready, you feel so much bigger and so much less fearful that you think that is where your power lies. Not true. The addiction to anger has brought the world to the state it is in: Feed someone's fear until they think the only option is to fight and you'll have everyone under the control of that addiction. The more you choose to hold onto your anger the more you feed the global pattern – and anger is deadly. The angrier you allow yourself to get the more difficult it is to stay in touch with your soul and your true power and the more you feed your fear. Like any drug you are going to need more and more to get to the same feeling and the hangovers only get worse. When you see how self-destructive your anger is, it becomes insane to carry on.

The exercise that is absolutely necessary for every day, every breath practice is to breathe into your solar plexus, "I Am." When you can keep doing that with each breath, you will find yourself expanding into true power which is the polar opposite of anger and fear. From the perspective of total soul truth you can then look at what the anger is really about and when you can be honest and look at the true nature of anger – which is fear – you can begin to claim your authentic power. The only way to free yourself from anger is to begin to take responsibility for it as your own response to life and to ask what it would take for you to stop being angry with yourself?

Do not give up on compassion for the sake of one aspect of you that is hurting. The answer to anger is to find compassion. Find the compassion for yourself and for anyone else involved in the situation because it is compassion that dissipates anger. Your Higher Self holds complete compassion for you and for everyone else. How would it be to look at yourself and the other person and the situation you are angry about from the perspective of your Higher Self? Step back into that perspective and you will see that the whole dance of anger is just another thing you have constructed to block your remembrance of your true nature, which is love. Truly, truly, love and anger cannot live in the same heart. Physical hearts cannot contain anger – they get dreadfully diseased and then you just have to come back again to try and deal with the anger next time around, so claim your Divine power. Do it right now and you will save yourself many lifetimes of frustration.

How do I free myself from addiction?

The only way to stop an addiction from being the power in your life is to engage deeply with what is the power in your life – you. You are the power in your life and for as long as you believe that you are not, you will be an addict. As long as you believe that the power belongs to someone or something else there is no way to be completely free of addictions and not just the chemical, physical addictions but also the addictions to control or chaos or pain or drama which so many people on this planet are running. Until there is a way to engage with authentic true soul power there is no way out of addictions. Your power is your true soul self. Your power is the Divinity within you. Your power is the essence of who you truly are and as long as you pretend it is not there, you will remain an addict to whatever it is you are currently focusing on.

To really claim that true power can be a lifetime's work – and turn into another addiction – or it can happen in a heartbeat. It can be as simple as making the decision to claim the true joyful power that comes from being silent and conscious. Breathe in "I Am", deep into your solar plexus and feel the expansion in that energy centre. Allow that energy to flow down your legs and deep into the earth. Imagine it moving up again into your legs, all the way into your heart and right up to the crown of your head. Feel what happens to your body if you consciously breathe that in. This quality is within you and around you and the more you breathe it in, the more you connect with it. If you can become quiet and feel that, it will always bring you back to your centre and you will always be able to use it to empower yourself rather than getting lost in the chaos of addiction.

I have real issues of trust. I can't even trust myself. What can I do?

The whole issue of trust is really about judgement. "I cannot trust myself" really means "I cannot trust myself because I got it wrong" and therefore "I cannot trust you, because you might also get it wrong" and mainly of course "I cannot trust God, because God gets everything wrong." Just sit with that statement and feel what happens in your body. If that is your truth you have run completely on panic your whole life and have never, ever felt safe. Without being able to trust that there is a perfect plan unfolding, everything becomes based on fear and chaos. From the depth of your being you know that this has to be addressed. There can be no journey if you are not able to trust anything so please do whatever it takes to change that mindset otherwise your reality will only ever reflect the chaos you fear and you will have to come back again and again to sort it out. The world has been run on exactly this energy and we can no longer sustain a planet with that lack of trust and the level of judgement it implies.

It is a very slippery slope to have got to a place where you feel you cannot trust yourself. If you do not trust yourself, where can you go from there? What is your story? What has happened that was so awful that you could feel so removed from the love of the Universe? What were your parents like? We are wired to look at Dad as God and Mum as Earth so if you had a scary or absent Mum how could you believe that being on Earth would be safe? If Dad was scary or absent, then God would be scary and untrustworthy and certainly nothing you could believe in or trust.

Now look at the bigger picture. You don't lack faith because your dad was scary or absent, you chose him because you needed to find faith, to have a lifetime where you could reconnect with that energy and remember to look for a bigger picture. Your initial judgement that God could not be trusted led you to choose parents who would play that out for you so that you could move beyond it. You also set up people all around you to 'prove' that the Universe was not worthy of your trust. You put your faith in things and people and they let you down. You trusted and you were betrayed. The question you must really ask here is what if the way things turned out was absolutely right on track and perfectly in alignment with your soul's highest truth and those people were simply allowing you the perfect opportunity to remember that?

The truth is that when you get to this place, the angels rejoice. This sounds like the kind of avalanche of terrible things that always signifies the time for a breakthrough and usually the reason anyone signs up for such an experience is that they have agreed never again to do life with a closed heart. This is a sign that there have been many lifetimes where you chose to turn your back on your true nature, where you were given a choice and you chose the path of ease and did not get to where you wanted to be. This time you said: "Please everyone, make absolutely sure I do not do that again. Please make sure I do this life with my heart cracked wide open and that I get to totally understand my true nature, which is love." Of course everyone agreed and signed the contract you handed to them.

From this place there is only one step and that is into surrender. Give up all ideas of power and control. Release it all into total surrender. Allow yourself to start saying: "Thy will be done. I cannot fix or change this so I may as well go with this flow and let it all unfold. I can no longer resist the Divine plan." Whatever you are living through, there is a plan and change is the only constant. What feels completely stuck will change and when it is unstuck and your begins to life flow you will look back and see all the gifts that grew in this terrible time of feeling as if you were drowning in mud. It is so often the beginning of every success story. The situation will change. That is the nature of the Universe. After winter comes spring and if you have done everything you can to try and change things and they are still stuck – stop!

There is such a thing as timing. You have signed up for a specific time to make absolutely sure you 'get it' and until that time is done, well, it is not done. So wait it out. In the meantime do something practical, like taking a deep breath. In the depths of despair the first thing that happens is that you stop breathing fully so while you are reading these words begin to breathe very deeply in and hold the breath for a count of three then breathe out and hold for a count of three. Do this a few times and see how the world already looks slightly brighter. More oxygen lifts your mood and your sense of wellbeing. Try it.

Another very practical step is to take some quiet time to look clearly and with focus at each 'negative' event in your life that has led you to believe you cannot trust yourself or anyone else. Promise yourself you will be completely truthful. Now, instead of thinking that you were stupid and should have, could have done something different, look at what happened subsequently and really allow yourself to see that each 'negative' event took you on a journey where you learnt an amazing amount about yourself and about life. Maybe it taught you about compassion, which we only ever learn by experiencing pain. Maybe it taught you about the strength you have inside. Maybe it gave you the perfect opportunity to find a way back to the light of who you really are. So was it a massive mistake or were you learning and growing and becoming the amazing person you are now on this journey towards the light? Did that event not nudge you closer to this place where you are now asking questions that are showing the way forward?

Please know that if trust is your issue it means that you came with a big purpose. You came to clear lifetimes' worth of lack of faith and trust. If what you set up is 'I can't trust God', step into the bigger picture and you will see that baby souls with baby purposes don't set that up. The Japanese say: "Who does hard things? He who can." You came with a big purpose – to explore that for yourself one last time, yes, but the minute you get it, you clear such a huge chunk of humanity's beliefs about trust and faith, beliefs that there isn't a Divine self within them who has value and all the qualities within them to live a life that is the expression of perfection. Trust is right up there with faith as one of the most important aspects of any spiritual journey and for every sentient being on this path towards enlightenment it is imperative for this issue to be addressed. If you can get to a state of totally knowing that there is a benign force in charge and that only perfection is ever possible and if you can then extend that to everything and everyone around you, including yourself, your life will immediately reflect something entirely different.

How do I make my life work?

There is a very short answer to this question and it is to change your perspective. Look first at what already works in your life. Look at the parts of your life that are actually OK and go back along the line of events that got you to that place. You might be in resistance at this point and want to claim that it is all horrid and none of it is working but stay open. Whatever your issue is, find what is working and acknowledge that and see if you can find even a tiny bit of gratitude for what you already have. If you are healthy, that is a huge benefit. Start with gratitude for that. If your relationship is working, feel appreciation for that. If you have good food to eat and friends to share it with, feel the joy in that. Be in this moment in your life and really look at it, then find a way to feel gratitude. It is trite but true: People who have great lives can be thankful but it is the thankful people who have great lives. Be in a space of gratitude and your life will miraculously change into something that you can feel gratitude for, which will bring more of the good life, which will bring more gratitude – but it starts with gratitude. Find the gratitude for what it is you have and more will be added to it.

Now take a look at what you perceive is not 'working' in your life. Pretend you have a magic wand and you could make everything perfect. Write down how your perfect life looks. How much money do you have? Where are you living? How do you look? What are you driving? Be very specific. What colour and make is your car? What year model? Furnish your dream house. What kind of work are you doing? How does that look and how do you feel, doing your dream job, earning as much as you desire and living in your dream house with good loving friends around you? Now get some magazines and cut out pictures that make your dreams more real. Make a collage. Use this to remind yourself of what you truly deserve. Keep these images at the forefront of your mind and give yourself a date by when this is going to happen and then go through the rest of the week as if someone has just phoned you and told you that all of this is on its way to you via a lottery win or whatever you can imagine. Keep the focus.

Then go out and give something away. You always have something to give. Start with a kind word and a smile if you really have nothing else, but do remember that everything you give comes back ten times over. The way to get your life to work is to give as much as you can at all times from a place of gratitude. The good you give and the bad you give – all of it comes back ten times over so choose what you want to experience.

Next, take a deep breath and hand it all over. You have ordered your food in the restaurant. Now it is time to have a drink and talk to the people around you and wait for the food to be brought to the table. It is inappropriate to go into the kitchen and tell the chef how to prepare the meal. You have placed your order and now you have to wait without trying to control it any further. All you have to remember is to know with a warm feeling around your heart that your bliss is on its way to you and while you are waiting it is also a good discipline to keep breathing in, "I Am Divine". If you stay open to guidance you will receive nudges and whispers from your soul. Your Higher Self will let you know if there are steps to take along the way.

How can I feel safe?

How does it feel to feel safe? You live in a body that is going to die and you do not know when that is going to happen so when your focus is on the body you have no choice but to feel unsafe. The only way to begin to feel safe is to place your focus on your true state which is that of a spirit in a body. Imagining your potential death and destruction makes you feel unsafe and it has nothing to do with your truth. The truth is your soul's vote which is that life is eternal and everything that happens is part of the bigger plan and exactly what you have mapped out for your highest good in each moment. If you can breathe that truth into every cell of your body, you can live your life from that perspective and then those feelings of being unsafe will begin to dissolve.

Everything is there for your good. Nothing has ever existed that is not part of a perfectly laid out plan for your soul to reach the highest state it is capable of and that highest state is reached through compassion – compassion for yourself, compassion for each living creature, compassion from deep true soul strength. Compassion does not mean being driven mad with pity and wanting everything to be different. No, this is the energy that can, with deep love, honour everyone's soul choices for how they need to grow and evolve. From this place of true deep compassion you can stand in your light and your power and beam it out to everything and everyone that exists with no judgement, enlightening everything, taking the clear light of truth into each situation. The truth will set everyone free and every soul who lives in that deep true state lights it up for everyone else. When the seed is planted in the matrix of the unified field in which everything exists, it makes it lighter for everyone else. Live from that place and you will never feel unsafe on this planet or anywhere else.

What did I do to deserve this?

Firstly – you absolutely did not 'deserve' this event in your life but what you did do was to come in on a contract. Every being on the planet is here as a contract worker. The cosmic plan that runs the whole Universe follows very specific laws and mathematically precise rules and your contracts fit precisely into those rules and regulations. You are God. So what did God do to deserve to have this painful event? You as your God-self looked at the video of all your past experiences and decided what you needed to learn and rebalance and what needed to be brought into order and you chose every single event in your life to help you do exactly that. You chose the people who would bring balance, healing and teaching into your life and who would best serve you to fulfil your contract.

Every event is an opportunity for you to learn something about yourself. Very often when you go through a massively difficult time, you look back and feel only gratitude as you realise that you have grown and developed much more than you could have imagined in that time of travail. Often these events are there simply to remind you that you are not a small, weak victim. They are specific reminders of the truth that you are and always have been a powerful being of light and part of the Divine experience of life.

So the question is not really what did you do to deserve this, but where did you step out of your faith that the Universe always helps you to grow and to heal? When you ask: "What did I do to deserve this?" you are playing at being a victim. When you ask: "What can this event or situation show me and teach me and help me to know?" you are claiming your power as a Divine being. Every single thing you deal with in your life is an opportunity to heal. There are no negatives, only opportunities to heal and where you need healing is where you sit with a judgement that the event or situation should not have happened.

Sometimes when your soul looks at your life path and plans what it is you are incarnating for this time around, you also look at the things that the planet needs to go through for its highest experience and growth and you choose specific events that would create healing for everyone around you or for the planet itself. Although it feels like a personal assault while you are going through it, if you could lift your vision to the next level you would see that you just took on a big piece of experience for the group. Because of your soul's willingness to go through this pain at this time, a whole piece of humanity that has not yet reached your stage of development has been shifted up a level. That is an incredible act of service and you were the only one who could do it. You did not 'deserve' it, you chose the experience so that the planet could ultimately experience more light.

Why do the people I love die?

Perhaps, "What has gone wrong?" is really the question here. You are on a spiritual journey and you have been a good person and lived your life focused on others. You do not steal, commit murder or lie and yet you are not covered in fairy dust and living a magical life, and bad things keep happening to you. How does that work?

Well, here is the answer. Your response to the first 'bad' experience you ever had was the one that set all the rest in motion. Your soul quest in this lifetime was to deal with anger and you asked every other soul to make sure you did not get distracted from that deep purpose. There have been lifetimes and lifetimes of working on this issue and so that you would follow through on your mission and not get lost again, you asked for help and everyone agreed. You set up a series of events to make sure that you had every opportunity to have all your rage buttons pushed so that you could deal with your intense anger. And who are you really angry with? You are angry with God.

Death is the big one for humans and clearly not something you can control. This is not just losing something or getting it stolen in which case you would have a person to blame. No, in this instance, it was God who created death and messed up your life and now you can never forgive God. This is what you are dealing with. When you came into incarnation you lost your temper and being an aspect of the Creator, with all the power that implies, you created chaos and so the cycle of guilt and rage started. It might be helpful for you to know that this is the last look at this one – for all humanity. The new earth cannot support these energies so they need to be cleared out of the earth's consciousness and you are playing your part in this.

The first step is to admit that the anger is there – and it feels like a shocking thing to admit. Every moment of passive aggressive martyrdom that you inflicted on those around you now has to be acknowledged as the pay-off you claimed because God made you angry and hurt you and you had to prove God's guilt. Almost everyone has some of this pattern of behaviour. You want to blame someone for your fate – and blame implies that someone owes you. There are even lawyers who make their living out of supporting people who need to blame and take. If you are blaming it is because you want to take something from the person you are blaming because they 'owe' you.

This is why people around you die. The only thing that can change that set-in-stone emotion of anger is heartbreak. Your loved ones have contracted to make you care and then leave so that your heart can crack open and the light can come in again. If you can keep it open enough for the light to fill it completely then the issue is resolved but most people let it open a crack and then, when they feel the pain, slam it shut again – and then think they have even more reason to be angry. Whether you express that anger as noisy raging or silent passive aggressive martyrdom, it is the same thing. Notice your own patterns of behaviour. Martyrdom is just as damaging as violent out-there rage. Victims say, "poor me" and are sad but martyrs say, tight-lipped: "I'm fine... but if you turn your back on me I will stab you."

How unbelievably different life would be on this planet if every child was taught from birth that we all live many lives and that everything is based on a mathematically precise set of circumstances that is organised to be perfectly balanced all the time. What looks like abuse or betrayal or abandonment is always a contract between souls who have to balance something in their mutual experiences and every single event is part of the perfect plan. When you hate, when you are full of judgement and anger, you come back to experience that which you hate and judge. If you were a misogynist in your last life, you would be female in this one with a difficult mother and a difficult daughter and you would have every perfect lesson to finally come to peace with being a female and with the feminine. If you were a Nazi, you would be a Jew this time, if you were black you would be white and on and on. If everyone could have compassion in each moment instead of rage, if everyone could forgive themselves and forgive God, the possibility of heaven on earth would instantly manifest and finally it would all come back to balance and all would come to a place of ease and grace and peace.

Nothing that has happened in your life was a mistake. God didn't mess up. You didn't mess up. It was all just an opportunity to shift the energy from hate and rage to love, acceptance and compassion. Those people around you who have died and left you alone with your anger were your greatest, most compassionate teachers. Death, for humans, is the thing that is non-negotiable and what they knew was that if death wouldn't help you get this, nothing would. Your friends, family and loved ones who died were the ones who said, "I will do whatever it takes" and that is exactly what they have done. They have never left you for an instant. They are right there alongside you, urging you on. Would you be willing to let go the illusion of loss and see how much you have gained?

How do I let go of grief?

Grief, like guilt, is often based on a misunderstanding. When you are in deep grief it is about something or someone that you did not want to lose or something that has happened that you have not 'given permission' for. The stance you have locked yourself into is one that is in direct opposition to Divine Will. You are basically standing like a solid rock of resistance screaming at the Universe: "Not this!!!" Grief often masks extreme rage that something happened that was not part of your plan. If you then add guilt to that, if you believe that you could or should have been able to stop it, you are locked into a rock hard place that it is almost impossible to escape from.

The first step is to try to find your way to a softer place where you can really truly hand it over. Make your mantra: "Not my will but thy will be done." Try as often as you can to find a quiet place and breathe your I Amness into your solar plexus until you feel that hard centre of yourself begin to expand and soften. Keep breathing until you find that it loosens the knot and then have a conversation with your Higher Self. Ask your Higher Self to show you the truth about your grief. Was it a huge mistake? Did the Divine, who runs a perfect Universe, get to your life's events and then lose the plot and start making incredible mistakes? In that case you have to know that the whole Universe is about to collapse because one Divine mistake will have a domino effect and it is all about to end with a bang!

What if, in fact, you signed up for an enormous level of learning, growing and teaching? Was the event that caused you all this grief the thing that has changed your life so that you may live a much bigger, deeper life with much more understanding of your own strength and beauty and much more capacity for compassion? Everything that teaches you more compassion is a gift. Every single 'terrible' thing that happens on the planet that allows you to soften your heart and feel more compassion is there specifically for you to do just that.

Could the grief you are hanging onto with such force actually turn out to be the very thing that leads you to greater acceptance, love and healing? Grief is simply a way to hold on to the past and it means you are not available for the present. It is one of the ways you get to stop yourself from being authentic when it takes over your life and your identity. What would happen if you let it go? Who would you be? What if you used the grief as the extraordinary gift that it truly is? When you begin to live your life as if all things happen in Divine perfection in Divine timing, even if they do not seem so at the time, your life will become filled with joy and love and will begin to blossom in incredible ways.

How do I find happiness?

The succinct answer to this question is: Find the thing you would die for and then live for it. Just sit with that for a moment and feel what happens. Ask yourself: "What would I die for?" Allow the answer to come to you. This will take you into a deep place inside yourself where your spirit and your essence and your soul live. It will open doors where they may seem to have been closed. Take the time to explore this question and you may find things begin to happen for you quite quickly and in surprising ways.

If you would like a more involved answer, however, this is a big topic and there is plenty to share on it. Firstly, know that if you are asking the question it means that somewhere deep inside your cells you know what happiness is and you therefore have the knowledge within you to find what it is that will bring it to you. If you can find that and live it, it becomes much more profound than just the pursuit of happiness. If you are asking for a sign or something to point you in the right direction when you are sad or unfulfilled or unhappy that means you are already on your way to answers. The fact that you asked the question shows that you are already on your path as a serious seeker and now the magic can begin. You may have heard the saying: "Knock and the door will be opened. Ask and your prayer will be answered. Seek and you will find." The fact that you are reading this says that your prayers have already been answered – although not necessarily in the way you are expecting. Perhaps you want someone to make happiness happen for you or you want things to show up in a particular way but that is not how the Universe works. The Universe works by giving you a feeling and when you act on the feeling, the miracle happens. Do you know that so many people have never had this feeling, this desire for happiness and so could not begin to find the answers, but you are asking and that is your sign. You need answers because you are sad or depressed or unhappy with your life. The fact that you have those feelings and you can name them and realise that you do not want to feel like that is a sign that your guides and angels are right there with you and have begun the work.

Happiness is what you strive for on some level but how do you know if you're happy unless you find what it is that makes you happy? So what is happiness for you? Look at what is it you believe will make you happy. How does happy look? How do you feel when you are happy? You need to be really clear about what it means for you so that you can know it when you find it. If you think you will be happy when you get married or buy a house or have a baby or become an artist or have more money or find a new job or go travelling, by all means do those things and every one of them will be a step along the way. Every single thing that feels good, that brings you peace and joy, that lifts you up, that lightens your life, all those contribute to your happiness but the soul truth about you is that you are already bliss and joy and enlightenment and those things are your Divine right. If you can remember that, you might very well find that happiness becomes a by-product of finding your bliss because when you seek for something outside yourself to make you happy you will only find whatever you are holding inside. Things and people come and go but your essence remains constant. So seek for the happiness inside of you that is you, by connecting with your Divine truth, by being true to yourself, by following your bliss and that will naturally lead you in the direction of what brings you joy and happiness.

Now look at what it is you believe is making you unhappy. Sadness and frustration and other so called negative emotions are part of the human condition built in so that you will keep looking for bliss. Those feelings are your key and your guide to shifting and changing what needs shifting and changing in your life. What would happen if you allowed yourself to feel those feelings? If you settle into the feeling of sadness you might find that you really have to engage with it and weep with all your might. Tears are there to cleanse and wash away stuck emotions, so engage with the sadness, cry for as long as it takes and then begin to notice that where the sadness was there is beginning to be a little kernel of peace. Also notice that when you engage with the sadness, it really doesn't kill you. The more you realise that feelings are not going to harm you but actually help you, the easier it becomes to let go of whatever you are addicted to that you use to keep feelings away or to block them out completely.

Addiction is a disease of fear of feeling. If you allow your feelings just to be there and you do not judge them, whatever they may be – isolation, loneliness, pain, frustration – then you have the possibility of moving forward. If you are prepared to sit with your feelings you will find that every feeling is based on fear of separation and that fear is based on the initial misunderstanding that when you left the Allness you were suddenly alone, abandoned and isolated when what really happened is that you just changed shape. You lowered your vibration to become physical but you were then and you are still the vibration of the Allness, the Absolute, pretending to be other than itself. It is just the same as it always was – you never left home. This is exactly as it was in the beginning. There is only one substance in the Universe and every single thing is made out of that one Divine energy. There is nothing else. There never has been and there never will be. Not even the blackest dark hole of being is anything other than Divine substance gathering information on what it is to experience. So do not be afraid of your feelings, they are actually amongst your greatest friends and if you are willing to befriend them, they will be great way-showers for you on the path to happiness.

There is another answer to this question and it is astoundingly simple. The way to happiness is to start creating it for others. Do unto others as you would have them do unto you. Treat people well, think well of them, speak well of them and an amazing lift will happen in your spirit. The concept of doing unto others is not a random floaty belief, it is a practical truth. The Universe is a mathematical construct and everything in it works perfectly and the book-keeping is meticulous. If you are not happy it is because you have not made others happy in the past or in the present. Check your life with a magnifying glass. Where and when did you say something about someone that was based on negativity and unhappiness? Where did you do something to someone that is now having the effect on your life of making you unhappy?

You and only you are the power in your life and the way the world works is that every single action has an effect so if your path has been a selfless serving path you will find happiness wherever you are. If your life has been grudging and bitter, you will reap that. Everything you have ever experienced has been because of a previous action you have taken or a thought you have had. If it is all going to come back to you, why would you risk doing anything that is not kind? You are not being punished by a punitive Universe, you are just experiencing a cyclical Universe. What goes up must come down. What goes around comes around. There is not a punishing angry God watching you. There is a hugely responsible Higher Self keeping track of every event and making sure that everything balances out in the end and it has to be meticulously balanced. Not one cent will be left unaccounted. Not one event will slip under the carpet. You can never get away with anything. Not one small thing. It is all recorded and kept track of and every bit of it will come back to you and not in small doses but times ten and more. If you hurt someone that moment will be recorded and revisited whether you remember it or not and if you are kind that moment will be recorded and revisited whether you remember it or not. Be incredibly conscious in every moment of your life about where your thoughts are. Be aware of what you are saying. Do not do anything that you would not like done to you because it will come back to you.

That is how the Universe was set up to work. Be kind, be thoughtful, be caring – but never in a martyring way. Do it with a glad and expectant heart, knowing that it will all come back ten times and more, pressed down and running over. If you prefer to vent and be angry and nasty by all means do that but do it consciously and with an expectant heart, knowing that it too will come back ten times over. Just be conscious. There is no judgement on any of it, it is just the movement and cycle of life and it is always in your hands. You get to choose every event and how you want to play it.

Of course what you do and say does not always come back 'in kind'. Sometimes it comes back in a roundabout way. The more you give, the more you get and it very rarely works that the person you give something to is the one who gives it back. It often comes back from a totally unexpected place so let go of how or from whom things will return to you and just be in love and compassion and kindness to all things and all people and you will see for yourself.

Most people looking back on their lives would see that they were happiest when they were little. Children are full of awe and wonderment, they have no cynicism or judgement. Remember that you are a living miracle, your body, your world, the whole ecosystem, technology – all of it is miraculous.

Happiness is that state of awe where you realise that you are part of the miracle of life. See the beauty and goodness in everything and everyone and that is what will be reflected back to you. Be thankful for everyone and everything in your life because all of it is showing up to support you in becoming more of who you really are. Never let an opportunity pass to thank someone just for being who they are. Start living from a place of fullness rather than emptiness. Focus on the many miracles big and small that make up your life and you will see more of them.

Keep seeking your bliss and while you seek, be grateful for everything along the way. Know that your joy is out there. The fact you could even conceive of such an idea means that it is waiting for you and at the right time the right thing will hit you over the head and stun you with its blindingly obvious light. When you get over the shock and think you have finally arrived, please know that there is no such thing. The real happiness is in the seeking and it is ongoing and it gets better and better – better than any drug because you cannot overdose on it and once you know the feeling it will always find you again. Depression is called the black dog because it always finds you again even when you thought you had lost it. Maybe joy/happiness is the white dog because like a loyal dog it will also always find you again even when you thought you had lost it.

Once you've found happiness the great thing is that you can share it. It is a rare gift and the people who spread happiness are the saints and masters on this planet. They make a difference and they are worth their weight in the gold that they exude from that state of joy. Ascension is a by-product of joy. It is simply the fastest, clearest way to raise your vibration. When you find that state of bliss and joy not only will you be happy but you will help create heaven on earth for everyone.

How can I be happy while there is so much suffering going on everywhere?

If a beggar asks you for money you can give it to them, or you can step into your own Divine light and through being that light you will remind them that they are part of the Divine too. Just beam to them the light that you are and see in them the light that they are and if at that point you still feel like giving them something then do it, but first be the Divine being you are and let them remember that that is who they are too.

The truth about you is that you are not one person on the planet – your soul is not just focusing through one human being. Your current situation is your focus but in reality there are 50,000 aspects of you on the planet. There is the part of you that is male and the part that is female, there is the part of you that is starving in Somalia and the part living in luxury in Hollywood and there are parts being everything in between, in various places on the planet. There are not 7 billion souls on the planet, there are 7 billion expressions of one light on the planet.

If that is the truth, what are the chances that the starving child in Somalia is going to get why it is here? It isn't, but the part of it that is you, seeking, that part will get it. As you shift your consciousness into the light all 50,000 parts of your soul strand will be moving into the light with you, no matter what they have been doing or focusing on or creating in their reality. It is a big thought but it also has a truth to it that your body will resonate with and it might be an interesting experiment to feel for those beings. As you step into your Divine self, actively begin to allow that energy to flow into whatever might exist on the planet as parallel realities, as parallel expressions of you, as parallel expressions of the Divine. Begin to see how incredibly vast you really are and how what you do has an impact on levels that you have never really conceived of before. Take your imagination there, feel how it is if that is true, feel if that is actually how it works. Feel how you impact on all those beings as all of the soul strands link – not one body and one soul but many bodies as aspects of the same Divine soul.

Now feel if you can allow yourself to be happy. What do you gain by not being happy? How do you impact on the rest of your soul aspects if you insist on being in misery? Does that help them? Not a jot. Being happy is part of your job. If you can do it, so can all of the rest of those beings. So go and be as happy as you can imagine yourself to be. Live your life in joy and bliss and every other wonderful thing and know that in doing so, you are lifting the vibration for all.

How can I stop feeling the whole world's pain?

What you are really asking is, "How can I stop feeling pain?" So what is your judgement on pain? And does it make it more important for you to pretend it is the whole world's pain? Here's the truth: The whole world's pain is not your business. You don't even know if what others feel is pain. You are simply filtering it through your own experiences and saying that if it happened to you it would be painful but you don't truly know how anybody else feels or how they are processing what they are experiencing.

Are you so full of judgement when you look at the world that all you can see is pain? Are you so locked into your position that you are projecting every single bit of who you are and your judgement onto everything that exists around you? You are looking at a world created by a Divine being and refusing to see the truth. How would you need to be and how would you need to see yourself, so that you can change that? Take a step out of your own pain – which you are projecting all around you – and ask the question: "Is this real and why have I created this?" Begin to understand that every bit of discomfort in your life, in your body, in your world is not the world's pain but your pain, and your pain is guilt looking for punishment.

So why are you guilty, what have you done, at which moment did you step out of your Divine self and manage to do something so wrong that the whole world needs to suffer to sort out that guilt? Guilt is the furthest removed from divinity, it is not true, it is a misunderstanding. Guilt is a total stepping out of your truth, out of your Divine self, into a place where suddenly you were the bit of the Creator that managed to screw up the perfection of the plan. Is that really true? If not, do whatever it takes to release yourself from that feeling because it is the greatest lie humanity was ever fed and has kept you from knowing the truth about your divinity. The most effective way to keep someone from being in their authentic power is to make them believe they are guilty. If you are guilty you can be completely controlled in every small aspect of your reality – and maybe you are not even locked up physically but you might as well be because you have no freedom. If guilt is the opposite of freedom find a way to reconnect with your Divine self which is absolutely, utterly and totally free all the time. Find a way to be that and give up on the whole idea of guilt.

If you are feeling the whole world's pain it is because you are a sensitive being and an empath and it is one of the choices you made before you came. The lesson is to have compassion and use it to heal whatever you can feel. The only pain you ever feel is your own and if you can really let yourself feel it you can take responsibility for it and heal it. Whatever you are feeling is yours but as we are all one anyway, any pain on the planet belongs to all. If you feel it you can have compassion for it and you can clear it out of your system and then it is lessened for everyone. Pain is not there to teach you how to deal with pain. It is there to teach you how to heal it, so every time a new layer comes up look at it and let it go and in the letting go you have just taken another piece of humanity's pain and removed it from the matrix and all of humanity has just had its vibration lifted. All pain can be healed by claiming ongoingly: "I'm sorry, please forgive me, I love you, thank you."

Is there a way to experience all the good bits in life without the crappy bits?

Firstly, crappy implies judgement. You signed up for the whole thing. You signed up for it all for your highest good and the bits you are deeming crappy are in fact exactly what you set up so that you could be kept on track, on purpose for your highest good in the most perfect way. Even the bits you say are not what you want were set up by you, for you, for your highest good. Even though you think you didn't choose them, everything was set up by you so look at the so-called the crappy bits and ask what is this moment or this situation or this event really for? What if it is, in fact, a gift? Could you look at it differently then?

Say your car breaks down and you are sitting by the side of the road getting upset or angry or annoyed. It might be uncomfortable – but what if it is still perfect? You see, you are so much bigger than you think you are. You are not a little person having small experiences. Your soul decided that you needed to be in whatever situation you are in at every given moment. In the car analogy, your soul committed eons ago to be in that exact spot at that exact moment so that you could do a particular thing. Your energy was required there to be whatever it needed to be for the earth, the stars, the person who drove past you. You don't have to know the reason for it all, you just have to be in the moment acknowledging it. Each moment is God's perfect moment, for the good of the planet, for the good of the Divine, for the good of the Allness, for the gift that you are being in that moment, the profoundly beloved gift.

The moment a human begins to wake up, to become conscious, something happens that sets him on a path that is not just about the sensory experience and as soon as that conscious journey begins the whole idea of pain becomes redundant. Until that shift begins the pain or 'crappy bits' of life have to be there to remind you what you are actually doing here. You are here to have the experience of forgetting that you are Divine as an experiment to see what it would take to remind you again. There are many planets where the beings have never forgotten who they are and there are also planets where the density is so deep that it will take many ages for the beings to start waking up. Earth is on the golden middle way where you arrive in a state of forgetting but you have everything you need to wake you up. This planet's blueprint of experience is for you to be given clues every step of the way so that you can remember who you are and come back to your enlightened state, your true state.

Can you be in compassion for yourself or another when life feels 'crappy'? Can you look at the bigger, higher picture and see that you are being given a golden opportunity to raise yourself above third dimensional living and open to a much more glorious state of being? The more present you are to the crappy stuff going on in your life, the more you acknowledge the feelings that they bring up for you, the more swiftly all of that can pass. It is your resistance that keeps the crap in place. What you call crap is just another way of the Divine speaking to you to show you where you are off-course, where you need to look at your life and make changes so that you are more in alignment with your own Divine truth.

Why do I always want to control everything?

How terror-stricken are you that you always want to control everything? How little faith do you have if you think you should be the one controlling everything? How far have you stepped away from your Divine self by the time you think you have to do that?

This pattern comes from a childhood where there was the threat of severe chaos and the only way to feel safe was to take control. It often happens with the child of an alcoholic parent or a difficult parent who had severe issues of their own which were never resolved. Here it would help to remember that the perfectionism and control was not caused by your parent but that this set of circumstances was chosen because your soul came to work on the addiction to control and the judgement of chaos. Remember that there is no negativity, there are only opportunities to heal. How would it be if you could step back into the space where you know that there is already a perfect plan and it isn't your job to make sure it is perfect? It will be perfect whether you run around organising or not. Yes, there are practical things that need doing in the world but it is less about what you do than the energy with which you do it.

Do the practical stuff from a clear space and see how things begin to take care of themselves. If you are constantly fixing and controlling and trying to make everything 'perfect', if you are continuously saying: "Excuse me God, you have made a terrible stuff-up but don't worry, I am here now", you are going to make yourself very, very tired. Give it up. It is not worth it and it is also not your truth. It is the opposite of your truth. Take a deep breath and stop controlling the Divine. The phrase, "Let go and let God" was specifically created for you. Make use of it often.

Why do I need to be right all the time?

When you were very small you took on the belief that this earth was a very unsafe place and that being here was somehow a terrible mistake and because you had made it, you could never make another mistake again. From then on you had to hold on tightly to that because if you were not making mistakes and you were right about everything and you could make everybody else think you were right about everything, then maybe you would not be so scared, maybe it wouldn't be so terrifying to be a small human all alone.

Really feel deeply into when that belief was created and ask your Higher Self to show you why you have to hang on to it so tightly. When did being wrong become just too terrifying? What would happen if you were wrong? What would be the outcome of losing an argument? Find a way to reconnect with your Divine self, to access the truth inside of who you really are. What you will discover if you allow yourself to really go there is that you have always been right, there have been no mistakes in the Universe, not one, not ever. It has always all been right and yes, you are part of that, so yes, you are always right – but not in the way you thought. Just start to relax into that.

Then take the extra step of exploring all those times when you proved to someone that you knew more and therefore should always be in control of everything and ask yourself honestly if that has served you in terms of your relationships. Has it helped you to create love in your life? Did it make everyone around you feel loved while you were proving to them how right you were? Your only real purpose is to love and be loved and that is the one thing that you cannot experience while you are insisting on proving that you are always right. How much more would kindness and compassion have helped you to love and be loved? How much more joy could you have experienced if you had been kind instead of right? It is never too late to change that. The fact that you are asking the question shows that you have awareness of it. It is never too late to see the Divine in everyone and everything, to practice compassion and to hold that space no matter what. That would be a much greater victory than being right.

What do I do when I am in resistance and how do I let go of it?

When you are in resistance the first question is: What are you resisting? Whose voice is the loudest in your head when you suddenly dig your heels in? It could be the voice of your mother or your father or a teacher or someone in authority.

Notice where the resistance comes from and how it feels in your body.

There are many people on the planet who have come back again and again to learn how to release resistance. If your whole life feels as if you would rather not be here, that you did not come to this planet on purpose, that it was somehow all a mistake, you are totally running your life on resistance. Maybe your life's theme is "You can't make me..." If this is the case you are going to have to work hard on connecting with your soul and getting your soul's vote on your life. Your body is always going to try either to control or to resist what you cannot control and that is the stance that is going to tense your shoulders and lock your jaw and give you stress headaches. Your soul is always going to allow and flow and trust the Universe to bring you the perfect outcome and the perfect journey to get to the perfect destination.

Releasing resistance begins with the awareness that you have locked yourself into a position and then asking yourself if that is really where you want to be. Why are you in this position? Is staying stuck and uncomfortable and in resistance what you really want? What is your fear of what will happen if you stop resisting? Resistance is usually about something you are unwilling to feel or face. What would happen if you allowed yourself to feel the thing you are shying away from? What if facing and releasing the resistance gave you access to your deepest inner truth and your deepest inner peace?

The answer to resistance is to take a deep breath, look up and breathe in, "I Am" because that is the energy that begins to shift it. You can try to resist and stay in your story but that is just your little inner child wanting to get your attention. When you are in resistance, breathe in "I am love" or "I am safe" or "I am truth" – just breathe. That is the key to all of it. The moment you do that you engage another part of your brain and you will find that your body, which has been locked into position, has to move. Breathing "I Am" deep into your belly you will find that you start relaxing into the situation you are in.

The moment you choose to stop resisting and connect with your I Amness, suddenly all your angels and guides will be there for you. Suddenly the air around you will be humming with the energy of all your light support. This support is there for you all the time but it cannot vibrate at that dense hard resisting frequency so it cannot reach you if you are locked into position and holding onto everything so as not to have to flow and be at ease in your life. Breathe consciously and choose to go with your soul's vote which is always love-based rather than the body's vote which is always fear-based. Just keep breathing and breathe yourself right through your resistance.

When you get into any sort of emotional state you are not present and you have stopped breathing. Life is in everything. It is in the air around you. If you breathe, you breathe in life. The moment you breathe again, you are no longer resisting life. When you stop resisting life, everything flows. It is in your resistance to life that you block things. See the Divine in the situation you are resisting. See the bigger picture unfolding with absolute perfection and remember that you are a powerful being having an experience of limitation but that is all it is – an experience. It is not who you are. The more you train yourself to notice what you are up to and the more you remember to breathe consciously, the more joyous and flowing your life will become.

What do I do about the inner demon three year old that seems to run my life – including my finances and relationships?

Sometimes looking back at an especially stressful time it feels as if a demon three year old was let loose in your reality and you may look at the event and wonder who on earth that was who went berserk and created chaos. This is a very serious thing for everyone. There is not one person on the planet who does not have an inner three year old who bites sometimes (even if you put her in pretty pink dress) and she often seems to appear out of nowhere. The door opens, she jumps out, creates chaos, the door closes again and except for everyone around you looking shattered, you are not even sure what just happened... If someone had to tell you later what you actually said, you would think: "But I am not that person. I would never say anything like that!" That was your little demon child who jumped out. Everyone has parts of themselves that got stuck, usually through a specific traumatic event or moment in childhood, so there is usually a 6 year old and a 14 year old who also burst out inappropriately at times. The traumatic event could have been something as simple as a parent saying, "Not now, I am busy" and the child hears this as, "I am invisible and I have no value", and acts from that place every time the same feeling is triggered.

A very serious part of your spiritual journey is to constantly listen to those voices inside yourself and notice who is responding to stressful events or situations. How old is the person reacting or answering the question? Follow that thought. Why is there suddenly a three year old, red faced and enraged, driving your car – or spending your money? It is a good exercise to keep up a conversation with this little being and the way to begin is to take time out. Be on your own with crayons and paper and ask your three year old self to communicate with you. Write questions for it then using your non-dominant hand, answer as the three year old. Have tissues handy – this can be quite emotional. Keep going until you can promise to love it and support it. Keep talking and communicating with it. You will be amazed what happens when your inner three year old is allowed to express itself in a safe and loving space and once it knows that, it may be less likely to jump out of the cupboard and frighten the neighbours...

Why does chaos follow me around?

What an interesting idea! Nothing and no-one has ever followed you around that you have not invited. You have not consciously invited chaos but somewhere inside you there is a belief that chaos is the only possibility for your life. It could be that you grew up with chaos or that your life path has been full of chaos but this has everything to do with what you believe about the Universe and the way it is run. If you truly believe that there is no plan to anything and that all is chaos and random and without rhyme or reason, that belief will absolutely create a reality where it will constantly be confirmed. There will be no option but to be followed by chaos. You will attract it with every breath you take. The fact that the question arose says that this issue is now up for review.

The Universe is a constant mirror of your beliefs in each moment and the next part of this question is where did the belief come from? It is based on one of the basic judgements that was made when you first came into incarnation. If you looked at the moment of separation from Source and thought it was suddenly all chaos you would have come back again and again to explore that belief so that you could come out on the other side and see the truth. This is a big part of what everyone on the planet has to overcome in terms of their view of reality.

You are asked now to go back to basics and look at how every small particle of the Universe works impeccably and with mathematical precision and then very clearly and logically ask yourself if in all the galaxies it could be possible that you are the only bit whose plan went awry – that you, out of everything that exists, should be the one small piece that somehow does not fit into the perfection of the plan. Is that true...? And if it is not, what will it take for you to realise that your journey has been absolutely perfect and on track and on purpose and that the chaos you created was exactly what your soul, as part of the Divine, asked for so that you could once again remember that you were living with a judgement that was based on a lie? There was never chaos. There has only ever been perfection unfolding. The chaos is purely a concept and a misunderstanding that you created through your misguided judgement that somewhere the Divine was out of control and because you are loved you will be given every opportunity to experience every nuance of that belief until you change your mind. When you remember that the Divine creates only constant ongoing perfection, your reality will shift into ease and grace.

People who create chaos often have a kind of inner imp that creates the chaos because it knows that the next level is coming up. There is a computer game called Tetris where you fit blocks into a pattern and every time you complete a line it falls away and every time you get to the next level the blocks fall faster. When it changes levels and the blocks suddenly start crashing down on you it is very hard to stay focused and to keep them all going. It looks like chaos but it is simply the next level coming up. It is the opportunity to do it faster, to do it better. Here's the thing: You are always going to be on the edge of what could appear to be chaos unless you actively embrace it and joyously accept it as the next level coming up. Joyously honour your journey because it shows that you have actually passed the test. You can now be trusted to do the next level and there isn't a final destination, there isn't a 'there',

there is always something else to learn, always another opportunity to become even more, to learn even more, to go higher and further. You are always going to grow and change and shift and the chaos following you is only chaos while you are calling it chaos. If you look at it clearly you will see it is the unfolding of the perfection that happens for somebody who can move fast enough to deal with it.

A practical exercise would be to breathe deeply and take another look at the situation and see if you can see the perfection. Take every opportunity to say, "this is perfect" and the more you claim it the more you will find that the perfection will show itself and suddenly what seemed chaotic will turn out to be exactly as you needed it to be. It is also very helpful to be in extreme gratitude for the perfection of each moment. Claiming, "I love you and thank you" for each moment will bring more and more joyful perfect experiences until you will find that you have lifted your vibration right out of what appeared to be chaos.

I've had a terrible shock and been badly traumatised. How do I get over it and let it go?

If you are holding onto a shocking memory it is because fear locks trauma into the cells and sets up the belief that if it can happen once, it can happen again and therefore you are not safe on the planet. Here you have to take yourself seriously and know that post traumatic shock is a real thing and you MUST go for the appropriate help to release the shock from your body. There are many ways to deal with it – find a therapist, a counsellor, a technique.

If you are reading this, however, you might be looking for a more holistic answer to the question. Once you have dealt with the physical aspects of the shock, if you are still struggling to let go of the memory and the need to continuously replay it, begin to look at what it is you are actually doing because there is once again a judgement. The judgement is that a terrible thing happened to you which shouldn't have happened and in that moment God was not functioning, there was no Divine. If you are a serious spiritual seeker, at this point you have to ask if that could possibly be the truth. Take a look at what this experience was really about and how it served you.

Why did you go through this experience? Did you do it because your contract was to take on that part of the human condition and go through that traumatic event so that a whole part of humanity wouldn't have to experience it? Were you the one who fed that piece of information back to the Allness? Begin to honour yourself for the amazing gift you have just given to every human on the planet and to the Divine. You are the one who added that bit of the information. Well done, and thank you. The person who co-created that with you was the person who loved you the most and allowed you to do the thing that might teach you the most, help you the most, evolve you and grow you the most. Look back at the shock and see who you were before and who you are now, with so much more information, so much more knowledge of your own strength, so much more compassion for anybody else who has had to go through anything difficult. Can you honestly look at the event and believe it shouldn't have happened? Can you begin to see that it was such a supremely profound part of your journey toward the light, such an incredible lesson, such an opportunity for growth and healing and acknowledging the gift of who you are?

This is the truth of all shocks, this is why everyone goes through difficult events. This is why every human has actually set out to have difficult events – so they could grow. Unfortunately growth often doesn't happen from a really easy space. When it gets too easy you sit back and let it all flow but you don't grow and you don't even remember to go looking for the light so you have to honour the shocks and know that without them you wouldn't have started your journey. What a profound gift is it that you had to go through the shock.

I always seem to feel sad and heart-broken. What can I do?

What you are describing is a kind of depression, a sense of loss, a feeling of never being happy. Why would you choose such a thing? If you stretch a bit to find the reason it will become clear. If your biggest intention was to become enlightened and enlightenment is living according to your soul's vote rather than your body's vote, you are walking around with the perfect barometer built in. That draggy unhappiness or broken heart is most definitely not your soul's quality. It is entirely only your physical self taking over and the moment you become conscious of it you have the opportunity to do something about it.

The moment you give it a name and you realise that your heart-break is there to keep you mindful then you can check in to see what is happening on your path. Are you in bliss or in heart-break – are you taking the soul's vote or the body's vote? Where do you choose to be? Do you want to stay with the body's pain or do you want to take the journey seriously and choose to do whatever it takes to get back to bliss? It would seem a bit insane to have come this far and not choose to do whatever it takes to get back to the enlightened blissful soul state that is naturally yours so what a profound gift is this heart-break!

Instead of getting sadder and sadder and full of judgement on your state of heart-break and thinking that you will never manage to get out of depression and therefore will never be enlightened, stop and take a step back. Maybe your heart getting broken is exactly the thing you needed to start your spiritual journey.

Realise that the feeling only exists to give you a chance to start breathing in your I Amness. Be grateful for the feeling because it is so unpleasant that it will always force you back onto the path of bliss and love and power and joy – all those wonderful soul qualities that you actually came to practice in this lifetime.

I feel at times that suicide is the only way out of my problems. Will I be punished if I do it?

Every death is a decision that each person makes at a soul level, so essentially every death is a suicide. Whether you grow a cancer or you wilfully harden your heart till it attacks you or you are in the exact place where the brick falls from the roof, each person makes that decision to leave the planet on the day they do. There are no accidents and there is nothing that happens that is not part of the perfection of the Divine plan. Whether your sadness grows a cancer or you decide to hang yourself, your time is your time and if it is not your time then your attempt will not work and if it is your time it will happen. So no, there is no punishment for committing suicide.

The very idea of punishment is so sad that it is not surprising that you want to commit suicide. A Divine force that consists completely of love could not, in a million years, have as part of its love the idea of punishing an aspect of itself. It would hurt. Do you hit your hand with a hammer when you write a wrong word? No, that would be insane, so where does the idea come from that the Divine would take a hammer to any part of itself? You are a perfect part of the Divine and there never has been any part of any of the system that was punitive. The Divine loves you – not just loves you, but is you. The more you can remember that and breathe it into your cells the more you will realise that only love exists. There is nothing else. There is nothing else in all the Universe. There is only love and no matter which way you stretch it, all you will find is love. Every single particle of everything is made up of love and it does not matter what the 'reality' looks like, the energy is still only love and perfection unfolding. Keep breathing that in and you will find that everything around you will start to feel lighter.

Instead of choosing to kill yourself today, choose instead to spend today only feeling love and extending that love through each of your energy centres. Focus on your base chakra and feel that vibrant red energy pulsing at the base of your spine and from that pulsing full energy, start beaming love in waves right around the planet. Then move your focus to your sacral chakra, above your pubic bone, and imagine an orange light pulsing. Make that light as bright as you can and from there send waves of love around the planet. Move your focus to your solar plexus, two inches above your navel, and imagine a yellow light pulsing. Make it as bright as you can and send waves of love from that energy centre, right around the planet. You are forming a rainbow that is folding itself around the planet.

Move your focus to your heart and imagine a green light pulsating from your heart and send waves of love from your heart to the heart of every living thing and keep the love flowing out. Remember that the planet is round so all this love you are sending out is coming back to you. With each breath you are absorbing love and sending it out. Now move your focus to your throat and feel a blue light pulsing and from that energy centre send love around the planet, peaceful beautiful blue wrapped around the planet and pulsing with love. Move your focus to your third eye, between your eyebrows, and send a deep indigo wave of love around the planet then move your focus to the top of your head and send a beautiful wave of violet love around the planet and see it wrapped in the rainbow of love you have created. That rainbow is pouring into you and filling every cell of your body with all the combined colours creating bright white light in every particle of you. Feel that expansion of love and light and hold it for as long as you need to.

And maybe if you have not killed yourself yet – do the whole thing again tomorrow...

Why is my body betraying me?

If you can step back into the knowing that your body is congealed spirit you will see that it cannot be anything other than the part of you that is doing your will. Your body is not separate from your essence. Your body is your essence made manifest in physical reality, it is the bit keeping you grounded on the earth, doing what you have come here to do. When you really integrate the concept of body and soul as one thing it is like asking why your soul is betraying you. It is not possible.

Your body can however be hurting to tell you something. It can be showing you that you've reneged on it, stepped out of it and treated it as if it is not spirit and not Divine. Take that Divine energy and step it back into your body and remember that there are not two things – body and spirit – your body is simply the highest aspect of you that has lowered its vibration into a solid physical form so that you can be and do everything you are here on this planet to be and do. There isn't a 'you' and a 'body', there is simply a body as you.

The higher your vibration goes the more you have to be very clear and conscious that your body is your vehicle and it is going with you into the light this time. Your body is part of the Ascension process and that is what is different this time because in the past you have had to leave your body in order to ascend. Your body knows this can happen as you have done it before on other planets but as part of the human experience here on earth you have forgotten that and must remember again. Take back the knowledge that every cell is Divine. Be that Divine light in every cell and the body cannot resist that energy. You will clear anything that is uncomfortable in your body, from aging to cancer, if you can fully, in each moment, stay conscious that every cell is Divine light made manifest.

Why do I struggle so much with my weight?

Everything is connected and everything, but everything, is based on judgement. You exist in this life on this planet only because your judgement brought you here. If you were in a blissful state of knowing that all was perfect exactly as it is, you would not be here, you would be exploring all the other realms in the Universe. So look at the judgement you have on your weight and imagine yourself as the parent of a child who is learning a new skill. Your baby is learning to walk and is struggling. After he tumbles over a few times do you, as the parent, have a wheelchair made so that he never has to fall again? Of course not. You keep helping him up to try again.

You have come to heal your judgement. This is the big skill you have come to learn in this lifetime. Weight and appearance are things you constructed to help you release the judgement and heal. Will you allow your Higher Self as your "parent" to help you do the thing you came to achieve? You struggle with your weight because self-judgement is one of the biggest issues you are dealing with. It is much easier to stop judging things that do not so closely concern you, but the body you wake up in every morning, the body you look at in the mirror and dress and present to the world, the body that the world judges when it looks at you? Not so easy to let go the judgement of that.

If there is only one thing in the Universe and it is all Divine and you are part of that, the biggest obstacle in the way of realising and living that, is self-hatred. You are beginning to know in your mind that the only way you can make sense of life is to look at it as if it is all one and that you are part of that. To do that you have to keep yourself in the equation, you have to know at the deepest level that you are Divine and that the Divine is perfect and to make that really accessible and understandable, you have to start with yourself. If everything in the Universe is love, when did you decide that your body was not part of the Universe?

How would it be if you realised that your weight issue is there to help you to ascend, that without it you might never have started the journey? How would it be if you took time to remember the lifetime when you had no problem with your weight and you knew you were beautiful? Look at how you treated others and how you forgot that your journey was towards the light and how little you achieved in terms of your soul's purpose. This time you very consciously decided not to do life as a beauty queen. You created a body that would give you exactly what you needed for this part of the journey. Every day, before you come into consciousness, before you fully wake up, check again with your soul: "Is this the day I will give up the judgement about my body and my weight?" and then you, only you, decide how you will look at your body and how you will feel about it that day.

Why do I suffer from allergies?

This is another question about judgement. When did you decide that you would resist or reject the thing or things you are allergic to? Everything on the planet is God, including you and including the thing you think you are allergic to. Remember who you really are. You are part of everything that is. Start taking yourself and your body very seriously as part of the Allness and use your power to bless everything that you touch.

Notice what you are allergic to. If it is a particular food, what judgement are you holding? Did you decide it is so uncontaminated and unclean that your body cannot absorb the Godness of that food? If you were born with an allergy, did you take on the judgements of your mother or your parents or your ancestors through your body? Perhaps you can trace your allergy back to past life experiences. An allergy to cats often has something to do with a lifetime in Egypt, and although that might be interesting it still only comes up in response to something that was seen to be a mistake, something you did or something that someone did to you. In that moment you stopped believing that there was a Divine plan unfolding and the judgement stuck for many lifetimes over thousands of years and it will continue to be part of your 'reality' until you are able to free yourself from the judgement.

There is obviously no answer that is quick and easy when you are in the throes of an allergy but if you really look at what triggers it and when, you are sure to see that there are specific emotions or issues that are more likely to make the allergy flare up. There really is only one thing to do with all life's problems and that is to work on your own issues. It is the number one way to sort out all the world's woes. Do whatever it takes to step back into your true power and feel for the truth of what these allergies are trying to remind you of. Maybe you really can just remember your truth and you will find that they will diminish. Maybe when you are ready to be at one with all that is, you will not need these allergies to make you feel special. Maybe you can just fall back in love with yourself and your life and that will begin to diminish them. It is truly only the judgement of this planet and what is on it that created these allergies in the first place and as you begin to see how they are helping you get back to the truth, maybe you can begin to thank them and release them.

Why am I so sensitive?

What do you mean by sensitive? Do you mean you are easily wounded? If you think sensitivity is a negative thing maybe what you call being sensitive is when you are actually giving yourself reasons to dislike other people because they have hurt your feelings. The truth is no one can hurt you unless you've said or done those things to yourself already. They're just helping you replay old programmes. Change your mind-talk about this. Instead of being sensitive and easily hurt be sensitive and easily moved. Be sensitively aware of others and their journeys.

In truth, how can you not be sensitive? If you were not sensitive, how would you function as a Divine being? Do you think the Divine is not sensitive to every single thing that goes on in every galaxy in every moment? Your sensitivity is such a huge part of your Divine self. Be sensitive. Listen to what the Universe tells you. Listen to what your heart tells you. Be sensitive to each moment and that will take you closer and closer to your Divine truth. That will take you right into who you really are. Your essence is enormously sensitive because it has to be, because that is your gift.

Your sensitivity is what moves you to look for your inner divinity and your connection to the Allness. Without that sensitivity you would not have had the impetus to start your spiritual journey, which always seems to begin with a feeling of Divine discontent. One of the big reasons for existence is to connect with one another and to have the opportunity to be of service. Without sensitivity you would not be able to be of selfless service. Sensitivity to others gives you the greatest gift of being able to know where the service needs to happen. True sensitivity is the greatest gift of the empath who knows they can be there for others without projecting their own beliefs and issues onto them. Often someone will give a gift or service they think the other person should have but this is simply a projection of their own need onto the other person. A sensitive person will be able to feel what the other needs and do that without projection of themselves into the situation. Sensitivity is a huge gift albeit often a painful one. The pain is only there to get your attention and to help you look at your sensitivity in a new light. Be grateful and honour your ability to be sensitive and it will develop and evolve like any other gift. Most of all be sensitive toward yourself. Treat yourself with utmost respect and care and love. Listen acutely to your inner guidance, the guidance that your sensitivity shows you through feelings, intuitive nudges and physical symptoms. Learn to use your sensitivity as the amazing tool it is.

I seem to spend my whole life running around after others and I end up resentful and exhausted but I can't see a way out. How can I change this?

If you are running after others because you are the parent and they are little and they need you to do that, that is fine, that is your job. If you then decide this is the only thing that makes you feel as if you have value or worth and you carry on doing it, then it becomes a problem. The trick is not to get into the needy stance of: "Please like me, please like me; if I serve will you like me?" and if you are already there then clearly you are living out a family pattern. The message you took on was that you were only acceptable when you were doing for others and being 'selfish' was a big deal. It was a word used as such an insult and with such power that it was the one thing nobody wanted to be. The truth is that it is the only way to be, because you are the aspect of the Divine focusing through your life and you have to take responsibility for that. You have to be the power in your life that looks after you. Nobody else can do that for you – nobody can bath for you, nobody can cry for you, nobody can do your life for you.

What would happen if you stopped looking after everyone else? Would they stop liking you? Is that really your motivation? If it is, can you see what a supremely disempowered position that is? If you are doing it because you believe they are not capable of helping themselves, can you see what an arrogant position that is? If we are all God in a body there is never anyone who is less than that and it is an arrogant misunderstanding to be constantly doing for others.

The way to change this pattern is simply to change it. Give yourself permission to say no. You are solely responsible for the bit of the Divine inside you and your job is to make sure that part of divinity is not abused or mistreated in any way so begin to ask yourself, every time someone wants something from you, if that is being kind to your bit of the Divine. If it feels light, say yes and do it with joy. If it feels heavy, say no and trust that there will be no comeback. The world will not end if you start to look after yourself. Can you remember how horrid it was when your mother martyred herself with sighs and exhaustion? Do you really want to inflict that on everyone around you? Please, for your own and everyone's sake, just stop.

Will they really fall apart? Will they really stop existing, will they die if you don't do for them? How would it be if you claimed your Divine self fully, in every cell of your body, and all you could then be is that energy in their life, holding a space where the Divine in you takes full responsibility for you and you beam that out to everybody else? You will be doing for others in a way that is so powerful and so valuable, in a way that allows you to feel your value and your worth, in a way that doing for others is the body's response to a soul that knows it is a powerful healer.

This is the magenta way of doing life. Magenta reminds you that you are a human being not a human doing, and in being the magenta light which is the light of your soul star on the planet, everybody else gets what they need without you having to lift a finger. Magenta is the colour of Divine love, the love that encompasses everything and everyone. It is all anyone ever truly wants or needs and all you have to do is be that. A practical application would be to imagine beautiful magenta light above your crown pouring into your heart and then that light beaming out so that whoever steps into your sphere receives it. It is very helpful when you have children who want and want and want. What they are actually trying to do is just draw your energy out. If you can turn your body towards them and allow that light to flow through from your heart to their heart you will find they instantly get what they need and they will be fine. They will stop needing anything from you. You can even do this with the adults in your life. When somebody wants something if you drop your head and turn away they will carry on wanting and keep trying to draw the energy out. If instead you can fully square your shoulders, turn towards the person, make eye contact and imagine that magenta light pouring in from the top of your crown, down your spine, into your heart and out through your heart at them, you will find that they will instantly get what they really wanted – which was never actually about you – and will stop trying to pull it out of you. Try it, it works.

Why do I constantly feel overwhelmed?

Overwhelm comes from giving out your energy inappropriately without putting anything back. Overwhelm comes from not keeping the connection with your soul, not keeping the connecting with your source, forgetting who you are in the business of your life and it literally means you are running on empty. What if, instead, you were to stay connected? What if you were to acknowledge your divinity all the time? This is a discipline and an exercise but it is incredibly valuable.

When you are in a space of complete overwhelm, take time out. You just need to keep breathing. Do you know how easy it is to stop that feeling of overwhelm by taking three deep conscious breaths? All you have to do is breathe in "I Am", breathe the words into your solar plexus, feel that connection happening and you will instantly be plugged into your power source again and you will be filled with Divine energy. It is in the air around you. It is in between the moving particles that make up your seemingly solid body. Breathe it into your solar plexus and remind yourself that you are connected to an unlimited supply of Divine energy – energy being the key word. It is an energy source and it will instantly replenish you and put you back in your power and clear the feelings of overwhelm. If you can do that ongoingly and consciously, everything in your life will change. Everything will start to have that energetic connection to source and you will find your life becoming easier and more fun and more joyful and more Divine. You will not need to be overwhelmed to feel alive because you will be living from a place of sustained love and Divine energy which is infinitely more rewarding and empowered than the drama of being overwhelmed.

Is it selfish to put myself first?

What do you think you mean when you use the word selfish? Are you saying that it is a bad thing or are you registering that it is the best thing ever? Which part of the Divine do you think you are responsible for? If everyone is part of the One, if there is Divine energy in every single person, would it not be insane to actually think there is more Divine in you than there is in another and therefore you should be looking after them and taking responsibility for them, and be doing for them rather than for you?

Of course selfish is the way forward, of course looking after you means that you are in such a strong position that you can be fully in your Divine self and you can hold a space for another person until they can find their Divine self. Selfish is the only possible thing anyone can be. If you are coming from a place where selfish means you have to put you last and them first I promise you this lifetime is not going to get you where you want it to. You are going to have to come back and do over because that is not the way. Selfish in the true sense is exactly the way.

All my life I have felt abandoned. I just don't know how to get over that. What can I do?

This is a process that could take a lifetime or many lifetimes, or it could happen in an instant. This is an issue that you have brought with you and for many people it is one of the deepest. When you first came into incarnation from the state of oneness you looked around with shock at your changed state and made a judgement that you must have done something wrong because here you were all alone in the dark and totally abandoned by the light of the Allness from which you had come.

What to do about it? First, go back to the beginning. Take your Higher Self with you and go back to that moment when you left the Allness and see how it felt. Really acknowledge how it felt to step out of the light and the Allness and into a body and into darkness and into being alone. This is a life and death issue for the body. When people lived in caves the only way they survived was by being part of a group so being on your own was literally a threat to your survival. Even now, no one can survive in complete isolation and in truth, there is no such thing anyway.

Now let your Higher Self show you the higher truth of what really happened as you brought your light into incarnation. All you need to do is shift back into truth, move into a higher space where you can honestly say to yourself: "Is this the truth? Have I been abandoned?" On a practical level you might well have been, you might have been the baby who got left in a dustbin, yet your soul never experienced abandonment. Your soul has always known itself as part of the Allness, part of the absolute, totally connected on all levels. You are still as much a part of the Divine as you always were and the judgement that you were abandoned was a misunderstanding. You were never not part of the Oneness. When your body is allowed to really get that as truth you might find that you can let go of the whole idea that you were abandoned and then you will stop attracting experiences that prove your belief in abandonment. You only keep attracting them because of the belief you have been holding. Once you remember the truth, that you were never abandoned and cannot ever be, that you are utterly and completely a part of the Allness, the concept of abandonment loses its meaning. Even though ninety-nine percent of humanity has had feelings of abandonment, even though it is part of the human condition, it is so deeply far from the truth that it is a very difficult feeling to access once you shift your vibration.

If that is the soul's truth why would you have created such an experience? It goes back to the first moment of coming into creation and the judgement that God abandoned which you then re-experienced from every single angle you possibly could and in that, you fed that information into the Allness: "This is what abandonment feels like". It was simply there to give the Allness the opportunity to feel and experience everything that exists – fear, abuse, abandonment, betrayal. Every single human condition has been fed back to the Allness, adding to its knowledge of itself as the Allness, as the absolute. The Allness had no idea about anything except for love. That was all it was, that was all it knew. Coming in to incarnation you had the opportunity to experience every emotion as an opportunity to feed back that information but somehow you got stuck in the experience and believed it to be true. In truth, nobody punished you, nobody stopped loving you, nobody left you. You were the aspect of the Allness that came to experience this momentary feeling so that it could be accessed. That is all. If you can step back into your truth you will find that it wasn't true, it isn't true, you are not abandoned, you never left home in the first place. Through each incarnation, each life time, each moment, through all of time you have always been and will always be just one thing – an aspect of the Divine, experiencing.

I have shut down my feelings because it is just too painful to feel. How can I learn to open up again and be safe to feel?

The truth is that one of this world's great gifts to you is your ability to feel emotion. It is one of the things you came to experience and to explore on this planet. As this is a planet of duality you tend to label them good feelings and bad feelings, happy feelings and sad feelings but the scope and range of human emotions is vast and complex and the gift is the ability to feel all of them. To block them entirely means that somehow you are wasting the gift.

Blocked feelings create all sorts of blockages in your physical body and all sorts of difficulties in your reality creation so it really is very important to do whatever it takes to reconnect to your feelings and there is a specific technique to help you do this. You will have to explore the feelings but you won't have to step back into them and you don't have to relive the experiences.

Allow yourself to look at your life as if you are standing looking at a screen and it is playing out in front of you. Ask your soul to be right there with you, to stand there with you. Begin to let your soul step into you and feel that energy filling you up. Now, watch the events that stopped you from feeling unfolding through the eyes of your soul. Let it feel with you and see with you what your story was from the higher view and as you bring the higher vibration of your soul into the negative emotion of the events, you will find that the lower vibration will be dissipated and it will literally move out of the cells of your body. It no longer has a hook and it can no longer block you from accessing your feelings.

It is very important that you reconnect with your feelings. It is very seriously part of your journey to reconnect with them and it is also part of the journey to not give them a judgement or a label. Find a way to not have judgement on what it was that created the negative feelings and in letting go of the judgement there will be a letting go of the fear of feeling and in letting go of the fear there will be allowing and in the allowing there will be tremendous healing. The moment the healing happens the flow can begin. The whole of your life will open up when that flow is allowed to happen again.

How do I stop old habits and patterns from running my life?

You have to be conscious and you have to choose to stop. So stop – just stop. Nobody else can stop you. This is a kind of addiction. Until things become so unbearable that having the pattern is more uncomfortable than not having it you don't have the impetus to stop but why would you want to drive yourself that far? Why would you not just stop and change the pattern, do things differently?

There are many ways to deal with destructive habits and patterns but the first step is to want to change. Truly desiring change means you have started the journey and then you have to take responsibility and do something about it. It is not always easy to do but start the process by beginning to pay attention to what you are doing. When you begin to do the thing you want to stop, ask yourself: "What am I feeling right now and how would I feel if I stopped doing this?" The only way to do this is to wake up and notice what you are up to. Stop letting yourself run on neutral. Pay attention. Be in the moment and notice. That is why therapy is so valuable because you are asked to talk about yourself which means you begin to observe yourself and notice what you are up to. Journaling has the same effect. If you know you are going to have to write down what you have experienced and done today you begin to pay attention instead of just blanking out and carrying on with your habit or pattern without being present.

Find something else you can do in place of the habit or pattern you wish to change. Begin to install new programming in your subconscious by actively choosing something different. It is not easy to create a new habit but it is the same process as breaking a habit. Break the habit of whining about your habit and instead create a new one, a habit of stepping back into your Divine self, of stepping back into your 'I Amness'. Keep coming back to gratitude. It really is almost 'fake it until you make it' but do it, because that is the way to start the new journey, the new habit, the new way of being on the planet. When the urge comes to indulge in the behaviour you would like to change, notice the feelings, notice the thoughts you have about it, notice the voice in your head that says, "Go on, I dare you" and choose to do something different anyway.

Little by little your pattern will start to change as you become more conscious. When you shine the light of consciousness on something it has the power to transform.

I've been betrayed, over and over again. How do I break the cycle?

The answer to this question has two parts. The first is your belief that when you left the light to come to earth you were betrayed by God. You came into incarnation from the Allness so that you, as the Allness, could experience separation, but in that moment, because you were in separation and you felt lost and alone, you made a judgement that you were betrayed and you have relived that event again and again to get back to the truth that you are still part of the Allness and never left home in the first place. Your belief was triggered through a misunderstanding of what happened. Everything is as it has ever been and you are still part of the Divine and always will be. You and the other person are both part of the Divine – so which part of God betrayed which part of God? How is that even possible?

The second part is that, because so many souls took on this belief, it is an indication of deep initiation to the next level of your evolution. If you look clearly at the story of Jesus and

Judas you will see that Jesus had to have the experience of being crucified to achieve mastery over death in his life and to teach Ascension. To do that, he had to have Judas 'betray' him to the Romans. It was a perfect piece of the plan. If you can look at every betrayal or what you feel as betrayal as an opportunity to take a huge step forward in your spiritual journey you can take the emotional response out of what you believe to be betrayal. It then becomes the gift that it was meant to be, it becomes the very thing you needed most. You can then see those who 'betrayed' you as the souls who committed to be truly there for you on your journey, the ones who promised to get you to where you said you wanted to be on your spiritual path and then you can begin to feel truly grateful for their gifts. When you get to that place you can begin to live from a higher perspective and you no longer need to attract the 'betrayal' because you already know the higher truth in your body. You only attracted it in the first place because you continued to judge it. Once the judgement is gone, it no longer needs to be part of your reality.

Why do some things never seem to heal, no matter what I do?

When you have a situation that seems to be immovable and unchangeable it is often an issue of timing. Human time and spirit time can be very different. You want something to happen now because you have to live through time that passes. Spirit is always in the now where there is no idea of time passing. When you sign up for things in this life from your spirit perspective you forget that time is going to be an issue and you think, "Ten years? No problem." Then when you are on the earth plane where time matters hugely you are horrified by time that does not pass quickly enough. When you have something you need to heal and you do whatever you know to do and nothing changes, keep going. It will change when the time for it is right. Do what you are doing to heal it then put it down and wait. Everything changes and there will come a time when this too will have passed.

Maybe you have come into incarnation with the intention of really dealing with the issue of disease. At some point in your life you contract a disease and when you do, you do everything in your power to heal it: You deal with the emotional reason for it, you deal with the diet, you meditate and go for healing and the disease is healed. Three years later the disease is back or some other disease appears. What you forgot was that when you decided to deal with the issue of disease, you also said you would do it for the group. So when the next disease pops up, instead of getting in touch with your soul's truth and being reminded of what you signed up for, you get angry and frustrated and stop believing that you have power over anything and you have to end up coming back for another lifetime on the issue of disease.

Stay in touch with your soul which always knows your true path. Do not lose faith. It is still working. You are just so vast and powerful that you also signed up for all the little ones who could not do what you are doing and you said you would do it for all of them. This is your life of achieving mastery. Stay centred and in faith and keep your eye on the big picture and really try to remember that the big picture is so much, much bigger than you can imagine and you are so much more than you can imagine and only perfection can take place. Please do that and give it time. Whatever it is, it is healing.

How can I learn to accept myself?

How can you not accept yourself? How can you not want to be the proud owner of the wondrous gift that you are to you? This is what you came here to do, this is what you came to experience on this planet: Perfect human, perfect expression of the Divine, magnificent part of existence – that is your truth – and the journey is to find that truth in the very cells of your being. When you do not accept yourself you are simply not living truth. You are living a lie, you are expressing a lie. You cannot with any kind of logic look at a Universe that is working with the most impeccable, elegant perfection and think that you were the piece that stepped outside of that. You cannot do it anymore. You cannot say that God created a perfect Universe, that the Divine runs a Universe of mathematical precision and "then it got to my thighs!" You can no longer do that. It is not true. Begin to be a little bit more honouring of the Divine in you.

First define what is not acceptable about you. Is it your body that is not acceptable? Is it your intelligence that is not acceptable? Is it your life that is not acceptable? What is it? When you have decided what exactly is not OK about you, when you have isolated the really big one, the reason you can never be acceptable, then please know that you have the power as a creative being to change that.

Take really small steps to start the process off. Sleep on the other side of your bed. Get up an hour later or earlier. Drink tea instead of coffee. Begin by making just the tiniest choices that are different and although it may not seem like a big thing some of the neural pathways in your brain will begin to change and you will suddenly realise that everything about you and your life is a choice and you are in control of all of it. The more you realise that you have choice, the more you can decide how you want to feel about yourself and your life and eventually you will find the you who is choosing to change and feel different. That you is so deeply not your body or your life or whatever you have deemed unacceptable. That you is so deeply Divine and so connected to the Universe that more and more you will find that not only are you acceptable but so is everything and that everything is part of the Divine and therefore perfect – even you – in fact, especially you. You will get the information in your cells that you are totally magnificently perfectly acceptable to the Allness. You are such a magnificent part of the whole that nothing would exist without you. How can you not be acceptable if you are such a supremely necessary part of all existence?

How can I learn to love myself?

This is a really important question. Without self love you cannot manifest a reality that will make you happy. Your reality directly reflects how much you are able to love and accept yourself so start somewhere, but start. You are a powerful soul in a body having a human experience and that soul is directly connected to the Divine source of everything. All your soul ever sees is your perfection. All you are is love. There is no other energy in your soul. The whole idea that you need to learn to love yourself is a complete mystery to your soul because it knows that it is love and that love is your essence. In the depth of yourself there is only love and the more you connect with that part of yourself the more you will begin to feel the truth of that. So go back and find out when you stopped loving yourself. Babies have absolutely no problem loving themselves. When did you decide that in all of creation you were the bit that was unlovable? How did that happen?

Find a way to make a connection with the Divine in you and let it feel to you how utterly beloved you are. Reconnect with your Higher Self and see what it sees when it looks at you. Have eye to eye contact with your Higher Self. See the awe that this being has for who you are, the love that this being has for you, the total acceptance of the precious essence of who you are. Keep making that connection, keep breathing it in. It is in the air around you, so breathe consciously. With each breath remember who you are and breathe in "I Am" and the more you do that the more your body will begin to get your soul's perspective of who you are. As you do that you will find that your soul's vote will be the one that counts, not your body or your personality or the little damaged child that can never love or accept itself. Let those not be the voices in your head that rule you.

Your soul is part of the Divine and can see only divinity. If you make every breath conscious and breathe in your I Amness, you will keep reminding yourself of your essence which is love and Divine perfection. So what is not to love? In the whole mathematically perfect universal plan, how could you be the bit that slipped through the net, that became unlovable and imperfect? How would it be if you too are part of the perfection and every single bit of who you are is therefore perfect? Just feel that for a moment. Everything in the Universe is perfect. That includes you. Breathe that in.

This question is going to be a work in progress for the rest of your life, but you can start with tiny steps. Start by just being decent with yourself. Do you treat yourself as someone who irritates you half to death? Is there a constant stream of abuse from you to you, with extremely nasty personal remarks about your looks and your abilities? You would never be so rude and thoughtless as to call anyone else the names you call yourself. Start by being decent and stop saying anything unpleasant to or about yourself. Every time you criticise yourself stop and say sorry and pay yourself a compliment. When you catch yourself doing it have the grace and good manners to apologise. Say sorry and begin to mean it. It is a very good habit to develop. Begin to be aware of how you treat yourself and change that.

Do it now! Treat yourself as if you are the most important person in your life because you are. Think about it...

When you have done something good, acknowledge it. Write a list of all the nice things you have done today – for yourself and others. Begin to do the things for yourself you would do for someone you loved. Buy yourself flowers. Have a bath in something that feels and smells nice. This is where you can honestly fake it until you make it. Pretend you have someone madly in love with you. You will be amazed by how others begin to respond to you. How do you walk and dress and feel when you know you are being watched by an admirer? Here is the truth. You are. Your Higher Self watches you all the time and loves you with no holds barred. Your Higher Self is constantly amazed by how fabulous you are. It sees you doing the whole human journey when you are actually an angel and it knows of the massive courage it took for you to take on this journey. It sees you as the most incredible part of Divine creation to have been prepared to come and do this life. It constantly loves, admires and honours you for the gift you are to the Universe. You are unique and important. You are beautiful and gifted and nothing in the Universe could have worked the way it was meant to if you had not agreed to be here now. So please stop denying the greatness of who you are and claim yourself as the most lovable part of all existence.

This is who your soul believes in. This is your true nature. You are love. You have never not been love. You have just forgotten as part of learning how to pretend to be human but the time has now come to remember and to be Divine. Just do it and your soul will support you every step of the way. Your soul has been waiting for this moment since time began.

When you can do this for you, others will reflect it back to you and your life will reflect all the love you have for yourself many times over. When you can do this for you, you will do it for others too and they will begin to see the truth about themselves. Loving yourself is actually the most selfless thing you can do. By loving yourself you are being of service. You are completely in alignment with the higher truth of life that everything and everyone is love and you add that back into the planet's matrix – which is no small thing. So, literally, for God's sake – begin to do whatever it takes to love yourself.

How do I learn to be true to myself?

How can you not be true to yourself? Have you removed yourself so far from your source that you are living a total lie? If you are being a people pleaser and feel as if you are losing yourself in the process, you just need to tweak your thinking a bit. The truth is that you cannot ever be anything other than true to yourself. If you feel as if you have lost yourself, that is an illusion. You cannot lose anything. You only have you and that is a truth so you are already true to yourself – you cannot not be.

If you believe you are not being true to yourself in some way, start by asking, "Who am I?" The list is endless: I am my parent's child. I am my partner's partner. I am a friend. I am a healer, I am a doctor, I am an engineer, I am homeless… Think about all these different selves and write them down: I am clever, I am capable, I am stupid, I am useless. Notice how differently you describe yourself to different people. What you say to your parents is very different to what you say to your boss or your best friend. What about the voice in your head in the quiet of darkness? When you have carefully listed them and looked at your list, ask yourself if they are really your truth and then begin to breathe into your centre, "I Am". See if anything changes. If you truly connect with your highest aspect, your soul self, the voice that says you are without value or less than perfect begins to quieten.

Do this as often as you think about it. Connect to your soul or your Higher Self and with all your focus choose to live from your soul's perspective, the part of you that knows your truth and sees the perfection of who you really are. The more you do it the more it will become a visceral truth and the more difficult it will be to live outside of your deepest inner truth. This takes time but it is so very necessary. If you do not do this you cannot be true to yourself as what you are being true to will be based on the lie of the illusion and you cannot be true to a lie.

I know I'm capable of so much more. How do I break through my limitations so that I can live the life of my dreams?

The fact that you already know that you are capable of "so much more" says a lot. If you were not already on the way to the life of your dreams you would not even be able to have that thought. There are billions of people on the planet who do not have that knowing and who have no dreams or even a conception of a "life of their dreams". If you already know you are capable of more and you have a dream that means you just have a few more steps to get there.

Find the voice in your head that says you cannot have it all, that you are not valuable enough to have everything you dream of and engage with that voice by very logically explaining that as you are a spark of the Divine you are capable of manifesting all your dreams and are truly capable of a magical life full of miracles. It might be worthwhile to sit with a piece of paper and with your non-dominant hand write down everything that limits you. Allow yourself to really feel the heaviness that all those old beliefs bring – everything your older siblings or your parents or your teachers said and every criticism you ever took on board. Write them all down with your weaker hand then with your dominant hand write the truth about you. Start breathing in your truth. Breathe "I Am" into your solar plexus. Keep doing it until you feel that golden light expanding inside you. From that place of truth and power, explain to your small self, the one who believes all the negative things about you, that you are totally Divine and that as a powerful being of Divine light, you are absolutely capable of everything you can dream of.

This exercise is not to grow your ego and it is not about being selfish or self-serving. If you can do this and fully believe in your Divine power you will shine so brightly that all those who cannot even conceive of their own light will get some of that light and will be able to begin the journey back to their Source and their Divine selves. This is your service to humanity – to expand your light and claim your incredible capacity to move beyond your perceived limitations and live the life of your dreams. Stay open for the magic, stay open to your dreams. They are waiting for you.

People say I'm psychic but I don't really believe it. Isn't it just coincidence or my mind making things up?

The absolute truth is that if given appropriate training everyone can paint and everyone can sing. Some might need more training than others but everyone can pick up a pencil and make marks and everyone can open their mouths and make sounds. Some have enhanced abilities and natural gifts and they do them exceptionally well. Training obviously refines their gifts but the gifts are naturally there even before they have any training. In some cases small children can do things that look quite magical as they are so talented and their gifts are obvious to everyone who sees or hears them. Psychic ability is similarly one of the natural human skills and there are techniques that can help you to be more open and aware but some people are just naturally gifted. They can see and hear and sense things without having to be taught how to do it. For them, training would also amplify and refine their gift. It is not unnatural, just as Maria Callas and Picasso were not unnatural. They had a normal human ability that was so pronounced and developed that it was seen as exceptional.

Somehow in thousands of years of following the Judaic teaching being psychic has all but been declared a sin so rather than being an accepted human trait it has been hidden. Many people over the centuries have been actively persecuted for having this gift so it is not something that is taught at school like art, music and maths yet it is truly just another ability. It is as normal as the ability to write beautifully, do advanced algebra, sing or paint. For those who are gifted with psychic and intuitive ability now is the time to claim that gift again and maybe to start teaching others how to develop it. Use all the gifts you have and shine! Stop hiding any of them. That just makes everyone around you feel small as they also have to hide their gifts in the presence of someone who is hiding. It is time to develop all your god-given gifts to the best of your ability and in so doing, allow others to discover and share theirs.

The People Questions: Human Relationships

I'm full of love but can't find anyone to love me back. How can I change that?

Part of being human on planet earth is to learn about unconditional love and so far most of humanity has only known how to love conditionally. One way to learn how to be unconditional is to attract someone who cannot return your love, someone who has no clue about unconditional love. Your soul's contract is to learn to love unconditionally, to love whether you are loved back or not but because you have forgotten the contract, you go into martyrdom and all you can see is that no one can love you back. You have attracted souls who said they would pretend not to remember that you are Divine and would pretend that they did not know how to love so that you could have that experience for your growth and for your highest good. To learn how to love unconditionally you needed to know what it was to have conditions on love. Those people played the Judas to your Christ so that they could support and assist you in fulfilling your contract.

Can you find some gratitude for their gift? Can you see that those people who could not love you were your teachers who gave you the space to learn? That is a great first step. Dig deep and find true gratitude for what they have shown you. Then read the answer to the question: "How can I learn to love myself?" because that is the most important step of all.

How do I find a relationship that actually works?

This is a big question and has nothing to do with the people you have relationships with. This question is only about yourself. Until you love yourself as you deserve to be loved you cannot attract anyone who will not, on some level, abuse you. Your partner can only love you as much as your energy field will allow the love in. There are absolutely no exceptions to this. If you fully believe in yourself as a Divine part of the Allness and therefore deserving of adoration you will experience that and the only way to have a relationship that works is to start with yourself.

You have to be convinced that you are lovable and this cannot be lip service or pretence. You have to work on this until the truth of it sits deeply in your cells, until each cell vibrates with this truth, then every relationship you have will reflect it. While there is any part of you that believes you are guilty of some unspeakable deed in any of your lives or that you are somehow flawed or just not enough and do not deserve love, you cannot manifest it. Start breathing in with every breath you take that you deeply and truthfully accept and love yourself, that you are perfect and you deserve to be loved and when you begin to feel it, all your relationships will reflect that. It all starts with you. It can only be about you and if your reality is reflecting anything less than that, do whatever it takes to get you to believe and live the truth that you are part of the Divine and therefore perfect. It is imperative that everyone gets this so that humanity can shift to the next level of evolution where love is the foundation of everything.

How do I find my soul mate?

You have absolutely found your soul mate. Every person who crosses your path does so on a contract to make sure your highest good is attained, to make sure your journey takes you to the light. That is the true meaning and purpose of a soul mate. How much more do you want?

You might think the Hollywood picture of loving and being loved is what you are seeking but a soul mate is actually a being who commits to help you heal, to help you step into the light, to help you be the highest, greatest, best you that you can possibly be. Everyone along your path has offered you that, otherwise they wouldn't have been on your path. Could you relax into that and acknowledge each one as the soul mate that they are?

If you do this there will be a moment when it becomes so real that any single one of them could be the one you spend the rest of your days with, so find the one who it is the most fun to play with. Really – find the one who brings you the greatest joy but know that you meet all your soul mates, every day of your life, all the time. Every day you meet another soul mate. Maybe there isn't one person for you – and why should there be? What is that need about? How would it be if you were so utterly in a state of loving acceptance of yourself that there wasn't a need for anybody outside of you to reflect anything back? If you could find that in yourself, everybody would reflect it back because everything outside you is only a mirror of what you believe about yourself. If you could be in that place with yourself you would have that energy reflected back to you from every direction. So be your own soul mate, be the love of your life, be the one and when you are that, very often the Universe responds by creating exactly that in your outside reality as well. The first step is to be in that space with yourself. That is the key.

I struggle with the men in my life. How can I access my power as a female?

If this is your challenge the most interesting thing you can do for yourself is to access a past life as a man. There are various ways to do this. You can go for a past life regression with someone who can guide you into the experience or you can just go into meditation and ask your Higher Self to show you who you were and what you were like in a particular lifetime in a male body. You have had as many male lives as you have had female lives and in this one you came in with a huge opportunity to clear something about the difference between male and female experiences. At a soul level there is no difference. Your soul is everything, neither male nor female, incorporating all the aspects of all the lives you have lived but in this lifetime you have a judgement about males and about power or you would not be struggling with them.

What is the power you want and how does that look? What is it you actually mean by 'power'? How does that work around the men in your life? Have a feel for what you actually know about being male and then feel again what it is that you are struggling with. Your parents were set up to do exactly what your soul needed in this lifetime so if you had female lives of no power, you would have asked your mother to do martyrdom to remind you to take your power back in an appropriate way in this lifetime. If you did power in an inappropriate way in some of your male lives, you would have asked your father to do that for you so that you could remember how not to do it – or to forgive it in yourself.

For women to be powerful they have to first empower men. That might sound counter-intuitive but the reason so many men are controlling and throw their power around is because the essential energy of the male is truly not where the power sits. The female has always had the true power – the power to give life. Women have been the truly powerful ones on the planet from the beginning of time and all the power struggles have simply been men trying to access that same level of power. When a little boy is born, a tiny little scrap of humanity, completely new, the true power is not in his own little body, it is in the hugely powerful being who created him, gave birth to him and now has to feed him to keep him alive. How is that an empowered place for him? If he comes in with absolutely no power, then from the minute he has any conscious thoughts he will try to get hold of some. What often happens is that he ends up trying to control and to take power in inappropriate ways. The real gift would be to empower men in a way that would be absolutely authentic for them, knowing that empowering them will ultimately create the most clean, clear, beautiful power for women as well – and then finally male and female will come into balance, in true and absolute partnership, with no struggle for power. If you are God and he is God, why should there be a power struggle?

There is exactly the same Divine energy in male and female and if women can bring up their boys to know that about themselves there will be a generation of men that will be the most beautiful thing this planet has ever seen. Those shiny men will create a space for women that will be equally authentically powerful and joyous. There will be the most beautiful balance in each being and in each partnership and then on the planet. It will bring the balance back to humanity. It will bring the energy back to a place of harmony where there cannot be power struggles, there cannot be wars, there cannot be any more conflict because each soul will honour and empower each other soul.

The truth is, you are not struggling with the men in your life. You are only ever struggling with yourself. Nothing else exists. Everything is smoke and mirrors to remind you of who you truly are and what you are here for. Your power is your truth. There is no real male or female power – there is just divinity and that is power and that power is called love. That is the only bit of reality in all of existence. All the rest is the illusion that you set up at a soul level so that you could remember the truth.

Why am I attracted to powerful men?

Like attracts like. If you are attracted to powerful men it is because they are mirroring to you exactly what you are. If you are feeling like the weakest link in a relationship it is time to be a little more honest with yourself. Relationships are always mirrors and you might feel as if you are the weak one in a relationship but that is simply not true. You are attracted to someone who mirrors your true self to you. Look at your judgement on power and what it means to be powerful or to feel powerless. Which side of the game are you playing this time and which side did you play in other lifetimes? What would happen if you were to step out of the shadow in the relationship and become the power you really are?

Sometimes you choose a relationship with someone who will remind you how to do life differently. If you were a powerful man in a past life and you used that power in a way that needed balancing, you might be in a relationship with someone now who will hold up that mirror to you so that you can remember how not to do it this time. The easiest way to clear all of this is to be deeply grateful for the 'teacher' who is prepared to hold up the mirror for you and when it is done and there is nothing left to clear they will change or they will leave. If you do not need to learn anything more from them or from the relationship they will not have to hold up that mirror and then they can either show their true self and be the loving caring human they actually are, or if they have other contracts to fulfil they will move on and be with someone who still has that pattern to clear. Every relationship, every request from your soul, every moment of your life is worked out in the most perfect way and the more you can believe that the more you will notice it and the clearer it will become. Once your judgement is gone you will never have to experience the event or situation again and you will be free to be truly you and allow others to be truly who they are.

Why do I struggle with my mother and the females in my life?

As so often happens, it was a judgement that started this one off. If you incarnated into this body on this planet and the first thing you said was: "Oh no, not that planet again, it's a dreadful place!" your soul, which sets up the lessons for you, would say: "OK, since you attract what you judge, wouldn't it be nice for you to go and work that one out – and let's make sure you get it on all levels!" It is your judgement on the earth that keeps you feeling separate from her and from your mother and from the women in your life so of course you would choose a mother who would be a challenge for you and her job would be to remind you of your judgement so that you could release it.

Be so very careful of this struggle. If you are female and your mother and all the females in your life are difficult there is a strong possibility that your previous life was as a misogynist male so you had to come and be female in this lifetime to work that one out. Now that you know this, take the opportunity you are being offered. Your options are limited: You can either make peace with half of the world's population and begin to have a lovely, peaceful, balanced life, or you can keep hating every female and come back and do over, but if that is your choice it will be much, much worse next time around. In the beginning you get whispers and if you don't hear those you get shouts. If still you do not listen you get full-on war to make you stop the judgement, so take the opportunity you have been offered and find a way to let this judgement go.

If you are male and hating one side of the population, the same applies. You have a male and a female parent and the genes of both genders so if there is one gender that you struggle with, you have just cut 50 percent of yourself off. One of the huge things you have to do in this life is to bring balance to both sides of yourself. If 'Our Father' is Dad and Mother Earth is Mum, you really need to get all this into balance. You cannot make your life work if either of these aspects are out of balance. If you cannot make friends with your mother you will also have difficulty with being on a planet which is archetypally female. You are going to struggle with being grounded and present in your life and you are going to find it almost impossible to manifest anything, including a life of joy and abundance. The same is true if you find all the males in your life difficult. Your female side is your vision and your male side is your structure and if either of those is out of balance the other side also cannot function.

Make friends with your parents so you can make friends with yourself, otherwise you cannot reach a place of real self-acceptance. Make friends with your Mother Earth. She is not other, she is also part of the One. This Earth, that Heaven, same thing. Male and female, same thing. Spirit and matter, same thing. Deal with this issue in baby steps and as you begin to love the little things it will shift and one day you will wake up and love this place and you will find yourself reconnecting with the Earth. That will be the day your mother phones and says she has always adored you and how sorry she is that there have been difficulties between you. It really does work like that. You can also do it the other way around – make friends with your mother and you'll start to make friends with the Earth. Make it easy for yourself, take little steps, love the grass under your feet, grow a flower – remember that this planet has sex and chocolates! Find the things you can love about the Earth then begin to say: "I Am, You Am, We Am – all One". As you do this with the Earth you can do it with your mother. This is the key – it is not actually about your mother, it is about the part of you that is her that you are negating. Until you make peace with your mother you cannot really reach wholeness within yourself. At a DNA level you are 50% your mother so if you say, "I'm never going to be like her" you've just cut yourself in half. Do not punish yourself for the 'sins' of your mother or your father.

Do whatever it takes to be happy with who you are because ultimately if you don't, everything is just more difficult and painful than it needs to be. Make it your mission to forgive and release yourself. There are many therapies and techniques out there to help you do that. By all means explore them until you find one that helps you shift this, otherwise your life as a spiritual seeker is not going to take you where you would like it to go. Start with small changes. Start with being decent to yourself. Remember that whatever you are struggling with 'out there' is your mirror and it really does not help to wash the mirror when your face is dirty. Look very deeply into that mirror and begin to be decent with yourself. Start by deciding to never, ever say anything nasty to or about yourself – and when you catch yourself slipping up, be decent enough to apologise. Begin to treat yourself more gently. The key to it all and the most loving thing you can do for yourself is to forgive your mother and in doing so, forgive yourself.

How do I stop others from trying to control me?

When you try to stop anyone doing anything, you are essentially trying to control them, which just perpetuates the situation. Rather than trying to stop them, instead let go of the issue and really look at what it is you are actually upset about. Do you truly believe that others have power over you? Well, that is just not true. Ask instead what it is within you that creates the need for controlling people around you. What you are doing is creating situations to teach you something or remind you of something or balance something in your life. This has more to do with your energy than theirs and the energy you are running here is resistance. Many people come in with an energy of "you can't make me" and the difficulty with that is that you will come back again and again and still not reach what it is you have set out to achieve. The bottom-line is that the moment anyone supports or helps you it looks like control and you go back into a stance of solid resistance which ultimately leaves you in a very vulnerable position. There is no action, only reaction, which leaves you paralysed and in a terribly disempowered space, with no ability to change anything.

Why are you so locked into that stance? It has nothing to do with the other person. It never has anything to do anybody outside of yourself, so why are you trying to control everything? Why are you basically resisting everything that is being given to you? If you look very closely at this you are also saying to God, "You can't make me" and in that you are resisting all your good, all your abundance, all your incredible gifts because you have locked yourself in. It would be valuable now to look very clearly at yourself and give yourself permission to shift that energy.

If you are feeling controlled, go back to the moment when you first started believing that another could control you. Go all the way back to when you first felt controlled by others and out of your own control and see if you can really feel if that was the truth or if you misunderstood something. Often these feelings come from something that you completely misunderstood as a child. Stopping a three year old from climbing on a table is not controlling it, it is keeping it safe. If you find a lifetime where you were tied up in a dungeon, go into that memory with your Higher Self and see if you can, soul to soul, get what that experience taught you and the other person. Go in Higher Self to Higher Self and ask the other person what the contract was. A soul never, ever sets out to damage another soul. The contract is always something that needs to be balanced or forgiven and if you are ready to forgive, the whole process stops. If you can forgive all the souls along the way that played the role of the controller and also forgive yourself for all the times you played the controller you will find that there really is no one trying to control you. If you can take the extra step of sending gratitude for everything that was brought into balance, you will find that all the contracts about control have run their course and there is nothing more to learn.

Why do I keep attracting people who abuse me?

There are a number of spiritual principles at play here. Firstly, you tend to attract what you judge. If abusers are the people you judge the most strongly then you are also saying that they have nothing to do with you and they are 'other'. Here is a spiritual truth: We are all one thing. There is only one energy. There is only one thing in the Universe and you are it and it is you and it is everything. So the thing you look at and think it has nothing to do with you is the thing that is going to keep coming back for you to look at until you claim it as part of yourself and part of the Allness. The first step is to claim your own ability to be the abuser. Who do you abuse? Believe me, you are practicing abuse or the abuser would not need to find a way into your life and the deeper you bury that part of yourself the more you will attract the abuser. By now I imagine you are feeling quite irritated that anyone could make such a claim, but read on. The fact that you are attracting abusive people means that on some level you are colluding with the abuse.

When you are between lifetimes you choose every event you are going to experience in the next one and if you had a life where you were the abuser, you would set up a lifetime where you would get to see it from the other side. This is not a case of being punished for having done something wrong but rather an opportunity to let go of judgement, of yourself as the abuser as well as the person abusing you. You set up everybody around you to make sure you 'get' whatever it is you need to clear or heal or understand. Abusers are not able to abuse unless you have actively asked them, actively created that in your reality so that you can get back to your state of Divine wholeness.

The key to this issue is that when you came out of the Allness into a separate identity and a separate body you took on a core judgement. When you left the Allness you suddenly found yourself separate, out of the light and in the darkness, disconnected, totally having forgotten who you were and where you came from. This was unexpected because when you were part of the Allness you knew everything and suddenly not to know was like suffering from amnesia. When this apparent separation from the energy of love and Divine light happened it came as a real shock because you had been so clear on who you were and suddenly you had this entirely different experience. You came into incarnation as a human and you experienced separation and the divinely loving being that was in you and around you had to let you work out how to get back to your state of divinity because you set it up so that you would have to work it out for yourself.

In your state of forgetting you made a judgement on how it felt and you gave it a label. In that moment you made a judgement that if there was a God then that God betrayed, abandoned, abused – for each person it is different but you chose one core judgement to really work with and experience in this lifetime and that was set up by your soul before you 'left' the Allness. That is the thing you've been revisiting and revisiting over many lifetimes so that you can get back to the original state of knowing that, no matter how it seemed, you never left the Allness. If your initial judgement was that God abused then you would set up lifetimes of abuse – partners that abused, parents that abused, children that abused, society that abused. You would end up in situations that looked nightmarish in their awfulness and the more you judged, the more you attracted those situations and the more awful it became.

When finally you reach a place where you can step off this wheel, you will realise that it was never the truth. In that moment you recognise that as you stepped out of the Allness, all that happened is that you had a feeling, an emotion, an experience. When that feeling, emotion or experience is processed and sorted and the truth is once again in place, you can no longer attract the abuse or whatever else it is you are judging. God didn't abuse you, you stepped out of the Allness to have an experience, that was all. You were the part of the Allness that had the idea that it would be fun to know what it would be like to forget your own existence.

Maybe you were the abuser in the lifetime before this one and you were looking at the video of your past life and you said to everyone around the table: "Will you be my mother? My partner? My children? My boss?" You created each one and you gave them each a role to play like a director casting a play. You set it up specifically so that you could get back to that sense of wholeness where you didn't believe in abuse and everybody in your life agreed and said they would do it, because they love you. They agreed to be the ones who would do that for you until you could get to a place where you could let it go, where you could remember that it is simply not the truth but just an adventure. God did not abuse you – you left to have an adventure. It was the judgement that created the energy of what you perceive as abuse and even that is not real because what you are creating in your reality is an opportunity to heal. Each person is here is on a contract that you set up and the contract says: "No matter what it takes, I will help you become whole. I will help you get back to that place in the light which is your absolute utter total truth. I will be the one who pushes so hard and I will do that because you asked me to and because I love you. I will push you until you become the being that your truly are, the light that you truly are, the essence of divinity that you truly are."

You are a soul in direct alignment with the Divine, having a human experience and it is your responsibility to be the carer of the Divine spark focusing through you and not let that be abused. Allowing anyone to abuse you means you are not taking care of your own divinity. The way to change this is by treating everyone – including yourself, especially yourself – with deep compassion.

How can I save my child from pain?

Firstly, children are not baby souls. They are powerful beings of light who came to learn and teach just like every other soul. They set out to have exactly the experiences and opportunities they needed to find their way back to the light and to help everyone around them also find the light. That is every single human's only purpose and whether they are big or small, they are having all the experiences that they set out to have for their highest good in each moment. The faster every human wakes up to the truth of who they are and what they are here for the quicker all suffering and learning through suffering will end and all will live a blissful heaven on earth in the golden age.

So how do you save your child from pain? You may as well ask how you can save your child from the human experience and the answer would be to cut his life short – that's right, you would have to kill him. That is the only way. Clearly that is not an option so take a look at the misguided thought that led to the question. This question comes straight from the instinctual primate mammal body and for that body, life is good and death is the worst thing that can happen. Almost every female animal on the planet is programmed to save her young and keep them alive but that is purely the body's vote. Your soul knows that that is the furthest from the truth of what is necessary for this being's experience. Your soul knows that this being chose you to give it exactly what it requested for its highest good.

I want to loudly remind you that you did not give birth to a baby soul. You gave birth to a powerful being of light, an ancient powerful being of light who incarnated to have a very specific set of experiences and it is not really your job to keep that from happening. Your animal body needs to keep that baby alive – if that is the contract, and even that is not a given. Maybe your particular powerful being of light only required a short time to finish what the soul requested from this incarnation and that means dealing with the death of a baby or child. Bodies go into shock and overwhelm but the soul rejoices that this being was in such a huge state of grace that they only needed to do a short earth-time journey to fulfil their work. From the human perspective he did not get a chance to grow and experience. The soul says look at the total journey and see how much light this being has already gathered that he was prepared to come and be this gift to his parents and peers, to have only needed this small piece of human experience to get back to his true state of light and love and bliss. When I have been with parents who have lost a child I have never seen the spirit as a child. I have always seen the amazing light being, tall and glorious and enlightened, who came in to have this last little experience on the planet.

The other thing you need to know if you are the parent of such a soul is that when these souls choose their lives and experiences the 'child' soul asks 12 times and the "mother" soul has to say yes 12 times before they agree that the child will come into incarnation and the parent will experience the death of their child. The souls always think that it will be just another experience along their path. They tend to forget how it will be to do that in a flesh and blood, hormone and emotion filled body. That is why the question has to be responded to at least 12 times.

How can you save your child from pain? It is not your job. You can love him and teach him skills and create a safe environment but the more you try to keep him from pain the further you move away from his and your soul's truth. Every being comes in with a blueprint of exactly what they need to experience for their highest good. Every soul knows exactly what it needs and your kids will set you up for exactly what their souls request for their highest good. If their journey is to come from a broken home or an addicted family they will make absolutely sure that they experience that. What you can do is to teach your children about joy and love because those are soul truths. Be joyous. Be loving. Do whatever it takes for your experience of life to be good and that will give your child much more support than anything you can try to do to make sure they do not feel pain.

If you want to do something extra, stand in your I Amness and use 'Namaste', which means "the Divine in me recognises the Divine in you." Use it with the full energy and power and essence of what it means. The moment you say "the Divine in me", you have accessed your highest vibration. If you can then add that it sees "the Divine in you", you have given your child everything it needs from you.

Why would someone push me away when I'm offering love and support?

This is a difficult one because at some point this person has decided that not only do they want what you have but that they want to be you. They're sitting with huge envy because they see your light and they have no idea how to find their own light or how to embrace it when they do. They literally haven't got the skills to step into that truth. Their soul knows that they are the light but they have no idea how to reach it. They are responding negatively to you and pushing you away to get your attention because they don't know how to get it appropriately. When you get angry with them for pushing you away they get something, but it is not the thing they're really looking for.

Remember to check very deeply within yourself what you want out of the encounter. Be absolutely sure that you are offering the love and support from a very clear space. Are you in any way trying to control the situation with your own neediness or by wanting them to respond to you with equal love and support or by needing them to feel beholden for the love and support you are offering? Once you have honestly looked at the situation and have let go of any of your own projections, if there is still a difficulty then your job is to take a step back out of the hurt or anger you're feeling and hold the space of 'I Am, You Am, We Am'. Hold a totally unconditional space where you have no judgement on it or on them. If you can do that, they cannot hold onto their stuff. Be in a space of clarity where you connect with your I Amness and you will have already lifted the vibration. Now see that in them – 'You Am'. The minute you do that they cannot hold on to their negativity. Next connect with 'We Am' and you will know that the other person is in fact you and you are them and if you can love all of it there is nothing left to learn from the situation and you will no longer need to attract it as part of your experience.

Why would someone I've loved and supported and been close to, turn against me?

Why have you once again activated that old program? How much of you still believes that there are situations where you could be abused by another because you deserve it? When you finally give up on the belief that you deserve any of it and you deal with your guilt and your belief that you are 'less than', it can all change and need never happen again.

What does the Dalai Lama do when someone close to him seemingly disagrees with him? Do you think he wonders why the person turned against him or do you think he just steps into love and compassion and holds a space for that person to deal with whatever they need to deal with? Do you think he even registers such a thing? It is not anything that sits in his energy field as a lesson he needs to learn or an energy he needs to let go of. He is so completely full of love and compassion that all he ever experiences is love and compassion back. With the deepest love for the other and himself he holds a space of total compassion for whatever is going on.

Only love exists. No one since time began has ever turned against you – no matter how it looked. There have only ever been soul contracts that were there to help you develop your compassion. This means that the person who hurt you the most was there as a perfect soulmate to help you develop your ability to express compassion. They were the one who served you at the deepest highest level and they were the one who enabled you to grow from the biggest gift of love. Thank them and honour them for the gift of love they were able to express. Understand that the more negative the situation appeared the greater was the gift. Who would have been prepared for that level of negative press? How much did they love you to do that for you, to make sure that you would find the love and the light again? Please, please, please have the great good grace to say a huge heartfelt thank you and you will find you no longer need to attract these situations into your life.

Why are people deliberately cruel and nasty to each other?

Notice where this question resonates in your body. Would you say that the feelings it brings up are linked to a judgement? Of course they are. There is huge judgement on this planet about how people treat one another. Humans are capable of extreme levels of horror and inflict it on one another endlessly. The judgement lies in thinking that it only happens out there: "How can they do that to others…" Every single human has within him or her the capacity for extreme cruelty. Some choose to express it and some choose to hide it but everyone has a shadow that, if it truly expressed itself, would be horrific.

So what do you do with that? The only way to stop the horror and cruelty on the planet is for every person to take another look at their shadow and claim it. Yes, you are capable of murder or violence or wanting to cause a slow painful death. If you know that about yourself and you know that in this lifetime you choose never to have to prove that, you are already closer to a place of enlightened compassion. If you are still up in arms about the things 'others' do to one another and you want to castrate paedophiles and punish criminals you are as culpable as the person actually committing the cruelty. If you can stop judging it because you are full of compassion for your own shadow and the shadows of everyone else and you have no judgement on any of it, then it can stop existing. You attract what you judge and if you do not judge it, it does not need to exist because you no longer need it to remind you that only perfection exists.

Why do certain people always press my buttons?

Why do you always have buttons to be pressed? Other than a belly button, you do not even have any so it is very clear that these so-called buttons were something you created so that they could be pressed. This has nothing to do with the other person and everything to do with you. You are truly not an automaton with no choice in what happens when the button is pressed. Your biggest gift is your free will and choice in each moment and how you respond is absolutely, without fail, one hundred percent up to you. When you have a person in your life that you respond to by feeling a certain way, that is your choice. You can choose to be angry and hurt or amused or vengeful or whatever you wish. All of that is up to you.

Your buttons can only be pressed when there is something unresolved lying within you which is calling for healing so when a button is pressed, take a deep breath and instead of reacting just ask yourself why you want to respond in a certain way. Did this person use a phrase that sounded like your older sibling or the most sarcastic teacher you had? Follow the feeling and you will find that it is actually not this moment's issue. This is an old pattern that has just presented itself again, so check with your Higher Self if it is appropriate to explode all over an innocent bystander for something that happened when you were six. Ask your Higher Self to show you what it was really about. Go back to the event when you were six and let your soul show how it gave you the event so that you could remember the incredibly powerful being of light that you truly are. Maybe you didn't remember back then when you were six, maybe instead you took on the feelings, took them inside yourself and made them part of who you thought you were, but there was a higher picture playing out. Let yourself be shown what that was. You now have the opportunity to see the perfection of the experience, the opportunity to know the truth of yourself.

You probably know people whose main job on the planet is to press buttons – not just yours but everybody in the household, everybody in the village or town, everybody in the world as far as you can see. They are master button-pressers. They will roar into a situation and do the worst thing they can think of in every given moment and, especially if they are your parent or partner, you might think it is your job to rescue the world from their chaos and the button-pressing gift they have. As a spiritual being it is actually your job to look at them with the most incredible awe and honouring of who they are and what they do and their gift to everybody who crosses their path, because how do you switch on a light? By pressing the switch.

How would it be if these button-pressing people were actually just switching on your lights for you, getting you to look at where you are holding a judgement? The original judgement was almost certainly of yourself and this person just mirrored to you the exact thing you were judging and offered you the opportunity to let go of the button. That button-pressing person was actually asking if you could look at them with love, compassion, acceptance and no judgement. If you could do that they would not have to press your buttons any more, in fact they couldn't press them if they didn't exist. That button-pressing person was simply your opportunity to let go of another level of judgement.

If you can thank the person who has just pressed your button for giving you the opportunity, you are free and no one need ever press that particular button again. Once you have given it up, it has no more hold on you.

Why do some people have such a big ego?

If you changed your mind about this and realised that every person you ever meet is there as an opportunity to become aware of divinity – your own and theirs and the oneness that links you – would you still worry about the size of their ego? What is it about their ego that presses your buttons? Do you feel they don't value you as they should? Are they looking down their nose at you? Are you feeling 'less than' when you bump up against what you perceive as feelings of superiority? Does that mean that their ego is out of control or does it perhaps mean that your feelings of inadequacy are triggered, and if so, who has the ego that is a problem?

To start the spiritual journey everyone needs an ego. If there was not an acknowledged part of you that thought it had value, you would not have started the journey. When you found out that you are part of the Divine and therefore utterly perfect and completely magnificent, you needed an ego to claim that. If your ego was so undeveloped that you just walked away because you could not conceive of the possibility of being a perfect part of a perfectly created system, that would have ended your spiritual journey until you found your way back again with a more developed ego. The problem is really not anyone else's big ego, it is always your own insecurity and that only ever comes from a misunderstanding and the extension of that misunderstanding to others. The misunderstanding occurs when you do not let yourself see that you and everyone else are perfect expressions of divinity, God in a body, and that your sole/soul job is simply to walk one another home, whatever it takes and however that looks.

If you are without judgement, if you are in a space of total love and compassion with yourself and everything that is, how would anybody's ego be anything other than something fascinating to look at and something to have great compassion for? How would it be if you looked at them and saw the little two year old that is pretending to be big? How would it be if you reminded yourself of what it was like when you were a little two year old pretending to be big? How would it be if you saw in this person with the 'big' ego someone who just felt so unsafe on the planet that they had to cling to that position, trying to stamp their feet and roar like a lion so that they could show everybody how big and scary they were, because inside they felt so tiny and disempowered and lost and bewildered? How would it be if they had been holding on to all of that in the hope that one day somebody would look at this ego-strutting stuff and see it for what it really was and treat it with complete love, compassion and acceptance, creating a space where it could simply fall away? How would it be if you could get to that place? Would you ever have to worry again about their ego, or yours?

My family and friends don't understand the spiritual perspective on life. If they would just get it everything would be fine! How can I get them to believe all this? How can I get them to change?

I suspect whoever is asking this question already knows the answer. No, you cannot change them. Why would you want to? They are expressions of the Divine. Why would it ever be your job to try and turn them into anything else? You are only responsible for the piece of the Divine energy that is within you. So easy, so difficult, but it is your job and it is the only one you have to do. It is not your job to care about what others think or believe. What if you just polished your own mirror and began to see yourself more and more clearly? What if you realised that all you ever do is look in a mirror that reflects exactly what you expect to see depending on what you believe?

The biggest part of the journey for any human is to be the Divine being that you truly are. If you are Divine then you are absolutely, utterly, totally, one thousand percent responsible for the divinity within you and it is not appropriate to allow the Divine being you are to be abused or neglected or treated in any way that does not honour that Divine light. If that is still going on in your life, look at where you still hold that you deserve it, because that is the bit you get to change. When you do, everything outside you reflects that. It cannot not. That is the way the Universe was set up to function. There is no other way.

The most transformative thing you can do for yourself is to constantly and continuously step back into knowing that the Divine in you recognises that everything outside of you is a perfect mirror of what you believe about yourself. As you claim more of your Divine aspect everything in the other person will begin to reflect that truth about you and if they don't change they will leave because they are no longer part of what you believe about yourself.

If you desperately need someone to change it only is because the part of you that they are reflecting to you is not something you are comfortable with in yourself and you are not yet clear enough within yourself to see the other person as they truly are. All you can see of them is what you perceive through your filters and what you believe about life, death, the Universe and everything else. Add to that a good dose of judgement and the picture is sufficiently muddied that all the truth has disappeared. Every single being in your life has contracted to be exactly the thing that you have asked them to be so that you can become the brightest light that you are capable of being.

Instead of trying to change them, how would it be if you just really looked at your own beliefs about yourself?

When you start your spiritual journey and you go looking for answers your partner or your parents or your children may find it really uncomfortable. You are now walking around shining a torch in their faces and often they will resist what you are doing and what you are going through. The truth is that all you are asked to do in each moment is to notice and not judge. Notice what happens and breathe, then if you can add a blessing or a bit of gratitude, that moment is suddenly absolutely fine. Notice the people around you and breathe and send them a blessing and add a bit of gratitude for that fact that they exist in your reality and you will be amazed at what eventually shows itself. The moment you stop judging everyone and just see them as an aspect of the Allness there is suddenly nothing wrong with them. They might actually become quite endearing. Add a blessing and a thank you to that and more and more you will find that people will start talking to you about life in a different way and eventually you will find that these people around you who you thought did not understand what you were about, are actually there to teach you and have kindly been waiting for you to open your eyes and see the truth of their part in your life. They have been waiting for you to catch up with them.

The Money Questions

Why do I never have enough money?

This is something many people think about constantly. The first thing to do is ask yourself: How much is enough? What would enough look like? This is where you see your patterns of addiction. An addict will tell you that one is too many, a thousand is never enough. Addiction is where you cannot claim your authentic power, where you give your power away to the addiction. If you are constantly focusing on lack it becomes a kind of addiction and the more you live in that energy the more addicted you become and the less empowered you are. Money does not show up in that energy.

Take a look at what you are projecting onto money – what is it to you? Chances are you never think about money in a truly realistic way. There is always some kind of projection onto money. For some it is survival and for some it is love and for some it is so real that it becomes their reason for existence. So which is it for you? Can you then see that the thing you have projected money onto is actually the thing that is not enough?

If money is what you see as love then there is not enough love in your life and how will you go about healing that? If it is survival, why are you in such a state of fear that you have to worry about it and how can you change that? If it has really become your only reason for existing then you will have to come back next time to do this lesson over and that is OK, but is there another option?

If there is not enough love in your life you have to look very seriously at how you treat yourself and in this case, pink is the answer. Here it really works to fake it until you make it. Treat yourself as if you are lovable and gather pink things around you – flowers, bath oil, clothes – paint a room pink. The vibration of pink is so calming and loving that all the energy of un-love will begin to dissipate. Treat yourself as if you are totally in love, as if you are totally lovable, as if someone is desperately in love with you and keep it up until the love and the money start flowing. Your true nature really is love so this is actually the easiest state to manipulate. Try it – it will work very quickly.

If money is survival find out where that fear comes from and do what it takes to sort it out. Is it real in the sense that you live in a war zone and your survival is at stake? Even then find a way to have faith that the right thing is happening and that there is still a Divine being who is in charge and who knows what your journey is meant to be and that your survival or lack of it is in the hands of divinity and your journey is perfectly on track.

Feel for the truth of your projection and look very deeply into what it is that you believe it is. The truth is that money is just energy and the clearer you become on what it is and what it is meant to do the more the flow will happen. Money is energy so it will always respond to your energy around it and the more you relax and remember that the more easily it will become accessible. Money is such a deliciously interesting thing because it is not real. That is the key to all your dealings with money and the more you can live that the more money can flow to you with ease. In the 3D world everything is geared to make you forget that and that is the greatest part of the illusion. If you think it is real and outside of you it will always be a problem but if you can remember how energy works and remind yourself every day about the truth and really live your from soul's truth and not the fearful bewildered body's illusion about what is going on, there will always be 'enough' and more. If you are living from your Higher Self, living in your I Amness, you simply will not be able to feel lack. Your soul has no concept of lack, it doesn't know what it is. When you are not anguishing and clutching you will see that there is an abundant supply of everything in the Universe.

Christ's consciousness was that he could manifest anything. He was utterly abundant and could instantly manifest anything and it came from within him. Step back into the connection with your Higher Self where every bit of universal energy is available to you in every moment and not only will you have money but your abundance on every other level will begin to improve too. Step back into the energy of being absolutely connected to the abundance of the Universe and 'not enough' will no longer be part of your reality.

Why can't we live in a society where we don't need money?

What is your judgement here? How do you think society would work without money? Money is such an elegant and easy way to create abundance on the planet and if you are in the flow and you understand that there is no separation between money and God, that there is no separation between anything and anything, then what is the problem? In practical terms it is unbelievably organised and easy, it's just that humans have given it a whole bunch of other values so that some can create lots of it and some feel envious about it and some actively push it away no matter how much they say they want it. It is not real. Money is simply another aspect of the Divine. It is Divine energy in action just as air is Divine energy in action, just as every other thing on the planet is Divine energy in action. When you are clearly living from your Divine self this will be reflected in how money shows up in your life. The more you allow the Divine to run your life, the easier it will become to allow money in. If you are a completely Divine being living on a Divine planet then you're not going to need money but until then, you are still a human being with a body, living on a physical planet and you still need to eat and drink and buy things to support your material comfort. Get over your judgement of money and start to see it as a substance that can make your life a gift of ease and joy.

How do I manifest what I desire?

When you are in a state of neediness or 'I want', you are vibrating at a low frequency and you are unable to attract anything. Your natural state is to vibrate at a level of perfection. When you say 'I need this' you move into an ego space and right there you are no longer being you as the Allness. Here you are, in your Allness and in perfection and then you say: "Actually, it isn't perfect because I need this. It would be perfect if I just had this, or that." Immediately, you've separated something out of the Divine, out of the Allness and then you are not in the moment, in the truth, in the reality of what is. When you are in your Allness and an idea or a vision arises from within that Allness, there is your perfect manifestation. It comes completely from being in the Allness rather than in a state of desiring or neediness and then there is no attachment as to whether or not the thing actually manifests. If you are really in a practical state of need, maybe you can't put food on the table, you have nothing in your pocket, then look at what you do have and give it away. Every single time you do that, what you give comes back pressed down and running over.

Can I be a truly spiritual person and also accept abundance and wealth into my life?

The only reason you exist at this time is to remember you are Divine. You are here to remember that you create your reality and do it in such a way that you get the most joy and the most abundance. The moment you step back into your true state and realise that you really are the power in your life and that it is all about you, everything changes. If you can really click your fingers and have anything you desire – absolutely anything – suddenly you will find that the desire is not so pressing. You only block yourself while you hold the belief that you are only human, less than perfect and that if only you had this or that you would be happy or perfect or more than you are in this moment.

If the truth about you is that you are the biggest part of the Divine – or that the Divine is the biggest part of you – then there is nothing holding you back. You are already spiritual and you cannot be more than you already are. That is your deepest truth and if you can accept that truth then maybe you can also accept the truth that you are as creative as any other part of the Divine and therefore be without judgement. Perhaps then you will stop judging yourself, stop misunderstanding who you really are and then abundance will become your soul right.

You cannot be Divine and in lack. What does that even mean? Breathe in your I Amness and know that there is no lack. Remember the joy you experienced in many of your lifetimes when you knew who you were and you created from that place of resonance. You did it in Atlantis, in Egypt, as an Essene, again as a Cathar, but the small knot of negativity inside kept undoing what you had achieved. Now it is time to fully embrace who you really are and with joy create wealth that cannot run out, or use up the earth, or abuse anything or anyone in its creation. Now is the time to create joyous abundance that will make everyone feel blessed when they become aware of your joy and your ability to create as it will remind them of their truth. Make your space beautiful so that everyone who enters it feels the joyous abundance of spirit in your space. Allow your own beauty to shine, be everything you came to be for God's sake and live abundantly in spirit and in the physical, in joy and in love.

Why is gold such a big deal on this planet?

This is a question for which the answer is still being revealed. The time for gold to be brought to its true power is still coming. Gold is an incredible conductor of energy and in your cells, in the depth of your being you have always known that. You hold the knowledge of gold in your deepest memories but the true information it has to offer has always been hidden. The time is coming for gold to once again be activated for its true purpose. What you are waiting for is not called a "golden age" for no reason. This is one of the great secrets that has lain waiting in the 'Hall of Records' under the Sphinx. It is also hidden in the depths of each human heart and with the true awakening it will become available again. The words of the song were a clue: "We are stardust. We are golden…" Another clue comes in this direct quote from The Golden Sufi: "And in our hearts we hold all the information that exists and a direct link to the Divine and to one another." You will find that the new children being born at this time have more of the truth about this.

Traditionally love is attributed to the colour pink – pretty in pink; Barbie; sugar and spice and all things nice; sugary sweet love and care – but love is really nothing like that. Love is great and powerful and creates universes and it is bright sparkling gold. Divine Love is a big golden energy that links straight into your solar plexus and is more to do with power than anything else. The moment you remember that bit of truth you can never see yourself as less-than ever again. You can then stand up and show that power and live it and be it. When you are in your absolute truth you are golden. You are ancient and powerful and bright sparkling gold. You have always loved gold because of its shine. The fact that it is the one thing that absolutely never changes or decays has been a perfect analogy of the quality of the gold at the centre of yourself. You too are ancient and powerful and indestructible and you have incredible shine and value.

The journey with gold is to find the inner gold rather than the outer gold, and sometimes, because that's the way reality works, if you really find and claim your inner gold, it will be paid in outside gold. You will attract the abundance and the riches and richness of what is available on the planet. The only reason gold exists and that you have a reaction to it is because it is a beautiful shiny mirror, reflecting who you are. If you could fully, fully, fully claim that for yourself and really understand it, you could step into the gold and become it.

Ascension: Growing In Consciousness

People talk about Ascension but I don't really know what that means. What is Ascension?

Ascension is basically where you become aware of what lies beyond the senses. Height, width and depth are the three dimensions that can be measured and in the third dimension life on earth is about what can be perceived with the five senses but spiritual seekers have always known that there are higher dimensions awaiting. Ascension literally means "to move up" and in the spiritual sense it means that the vibration of humanity and of the planet is moving from third dimensional to higher and higher levels. Ascension is not what you see in a children's bible with pictures of Jesus on a cloud. It is simply a lifting of energy from dense and slow and heavy to something lighter and clearer. It is moving from sadness to joy, from fear to truth, from darkness to light. It is just a tiny shift in perception and then another and another, and it is ongoing. There is no 'there' to get to, there is simply a continuum of ever-increasing lightness.

As you become aware of your soul and your soul's perspective you lift your vibration. Do this as an exercise: Look down at your feet, slump your back and think: "The world is a terrible place full of grief and sadness." Notice how dense that feels. Now take a deep breath, square your shoulders, look up and think: "Oh wow, I LOVE this place." Do it with enthusiasm and feel how light it feels. You have just lifted the vibration and that, in a nutshell, is Ascension. It is the lifting of the vibration from dense darkness to light airiness and the more you do it the more it grows and expands and then you begin to become aware that there is in fact another whole world around you that from a dense third dimensional state could not yet be accessed. As soon as you start looking to the light you instantly open to the other dimensions around you and in time that will become the norm for everyone on the planet.

It is unlikely to happen in one big 'whoosh' – although there may come a time of critical mass when the whole planet will experience a sudden surge of energy like a rollercoaster ride and all souls will leap into the light. You've done that before, on very many planets, and now you're here to be part of that whoosh into the light. That is the rush you've waited to feel for so long. That is why you are so tired. It still hasn't happened in the way you might have wished for or expected but the truth is, it is happening. Ascension is happening in ways both subtle and big but the shift is definitely on its way. The roll has started and it will continue to gather momentum. Ascension is where you realise that you are an ancient powerful being of light and that you have existed through all of time and that it has all always been perfect. The more you can access that the more the vibration of all humanity shifts and the more all can ascend to higher and higher levels of consciousness and beingness. The way to start the process for yourself is to find the joy. Find what makes you feel light and follow that as if your life depended on it, because it does.

How can we have hope for the future when the planet seems to be in such a mess?

You are the hope for the future. The fact that you ask this question says that somewhere inside you, you have already chosen to be part of the shift, chosen to be here now so that a hopeful space can be created. The fact that you ask this question means that something has already been set in motion that will create a new, hopeful, peaceful golden age. The fact that you ask this question means you are absolutely part of the shift in consciousness on the planet.

This is a serious question at a time when the news is not just bad but it seems to get worse and worse and with global communications it is available instantly and everywhere. The whole world is aware of what is going on in each corner. So – is that a problem or a sign of a world on the brink of awakening? What if this is truly a time where it is all about to change and everyone is being made aware of everything that is still hidden and slowly everyone on the planet is being forced to face their last hidden shadows? You would not see it if you did not have a connection to what it is you are noticing. The truth is that everything that you are becoming aware of has gone on since time began but living in Europe you might never before have been aware of what the Sultan of Brunei believes. Living in Pakistan you might never have known how women in England behave, but now everything is coming into the consciousness of everyone and the world is truly turning into a global village.

It would be a great thing if everyone could realise that all of it is about taking your power for transformation seriously. Everything is an opportunity to let go of your judgement. Everything is an opportunity to use your power to honour the choices of everyone of whom you are becoming aware. Did the woman who got stoned for marrying against her family's wishes not incarnate as a powerful aspect of the Divine? Was her incredible gift to the planet not to make all the rest of humanity aware of a belief that has been there since the beginning of time? Can you connect with your highest aspect and connect with her powerful soul and, soul to soul, check what the reality was in that event? Can you honour the amazing gift she was to the planet? Can you change your view about all of the "bad" news and check what you are judging or still guilty about or not forgiving to the extent that it still has to go on and on to get your attention? The moment all the judgement goes all of the bad news will stop. There will be no need for it. Use all your power to tune into a rhinoceros that has been killed by poachers – also check on the poacher. Are they really outside of the perfect plan of creation and is it OK for you to hate any of it? Or are you in fact being given a huge test to claim all of your power and simply with your powerful love transform all of it? You can do it. In fact, you incarnated for exactly that reason. You came to remember your incredible power as the Creator's light on the planet and you came to spread that light and ascend the planet. Yes, that is why you are here and that is why you asked this question.

The world is on the brink of a big awakening and as always when there is a big move, the old rubbish that no longer fits with the new house has to be gone through and thrown out. After many years of living in particular ways everything has to be re-examined and some things will be kept and some have to be discarded and there is always one member of the family who will fight tooth and nail to keep the old moth-eaten worn-thin smelly blanket that is twenty years past it's sell-by date. Humanity has now reached a point where all the old ways are being re-examined so that new ways of being can be created and lived.

The world is moving into Heaven on Earth and as a species, humanity has to do this physically. You are working through each of the chakras to become Divine humans, new humans. That is the next step. It is quite clear that the wave of light beings who have incarnated are standing on one side of the abyss and are holding the light so brightly while the dark side is equally holding on to the dark so tightly that this last battle is going to be an amazing event. It is happening globally. There is mass farming of animals in ghastly conditions, genocide all over Africa, bankers stealing, governments behaving like gangsters, mass starvation and lack and all the while the earth is heating up and behaving in unexpected ways. You who have come to hold the light are going to be asked to do a very big thing. You are asked to stare into the abyss and see all the darkness and not respond with fear or anything that reflects that darkness and to do that you have to be without any judgement on any of it. You have to be able to stand like the strongest warriors with only your love as your super power and hold that space until it is all over. This is not a passive love.

This is a golden wave of love that is going to cover the landscape like a tsunami and wash away everything that is not love. And first that has to happen within each person, within you.

If you go through each of your chakras you will see where you hold any old memory that might make you stumble into darkness when you are trying to hold that golden wave. For most people who call themselves spiritual, it starts at the crown. The moment you look at what you hold there you can see that historically humanity has tried to heal the world through this energy centre but because they only used this one and forgot or denied the rest, it did not work out so well. Think of the great move to 'civilise humanity' through Christianity where anyone who did not immediately allow themselves to be controlled was killed or crucified or persecuted. Then it is easy to see that if the base chakra is not clear, you can quite enjoy subjugating others and even kill them in the name of 'your' faith. If the solar plexus is not clear it is easy to use it to control others. And if the sacral is not clear it is easy to preach spirituality while abusing small boys…

All your energy centres are awakening and you just need to be aware of the traps, which are only there to show you where you are still not completely clear. For example, a Divine light being sees only as the Divine sees and is therefore incapable of judgement. The Divine creates and sees only perfection in every single event and knows that your free will is your most Divine ability and a light being will never, ever interfere with that. If you were to channel that light being that is the only energy that would come through. The moment you start to add a "thou shalt" into a sentence you have to know that you are channelling your own 'head girl/boy' energy and you are trying to control and all that has happened is that instead of channelling from the crown you have just moved the energy into the solar plexus where to stay safe you have to control everything. Negative crown energy means that you think your angel is bigger than the next person's and therefore you can tell them what they should do. The Divine being that you are channelling at that point has left the building. You are now channelling your mother or your father or your headmaster who made you do things you did not want to do.

To be part of the wave of golden love for the golden age – and it is a huge thing you have come to do on the planet at this time – you have to be diligent and notice every time you step out of the clear space of non-judgement where everything you look at is perfect. Feel which energy centre is hooked into the event and do whatever it takes to awaken that energy centre to its true Divine state. Claim your divinity and honour every moment and every choice with the total understanding that what you are part of is a humanity who will claim their divinity and change everything on the planet. Be in a place of total faith, total trust, total hope, knowing that it is coming. Hold the vision rather than looking at the chaos on the planet and getting into the negativity of it. Huge numbers of humans on the planet have incarnated specifically at this time to hold the vision and that is how it will come to pass. The journey now is to look at all of it with no judgement and retain the hope and retain the vision knowing that this is the next level and it is perfectly on track, on purpose, exactly as it was planned and set up since the beginning of time. There is so much hope for the planet and you are it.

You say we're all Divine and I know somewhere inside that it is true but I just can't feel that. How can I even really begin to believe it?

This is a good question, especially when your body feels quite uncomfortable even with the idea. When you're feeling small and your life is a misery and someone comes along and tells you to remember you're Divine, you wonder: "How on earth do I do that?" But the fact that you're asking the question says there is an aspect of you that is prepared to at least consider it as a possibility.

The thing is, as a human you are never really going to feel it – until you do. Until then you have to work incredibly diligently to let go of everything that makes you think you are not Divine. Notice every thought that says you have no value. Watch for every situation that makes you feel less-than. Watch like a hawk for the times when you denigrate yourself and then take it a step further and notice every thought that makes anybody else less-than. The only reason you will ever need to do that is because of your own feelings of not being good enough. Become aware of where your thoughts and feelings are taking you, then if you can remotely believe that there is a higher power of any kind, begin to sense or feel or imagine where it would be. If it is in the ether or the air around you, imagine that you can in fact breathe it in.

Take a deep breath and say to yourself, "I Am." Use your imagination if you have to. No one can prove or disprove that you are on the right track here – but what if it were so? What if the Divine was everything and everywhere, including in the air around you? Imagine you are breathing it into your solar plexus, two inches above your navel and an inch inside, and imagine that the air you are breathing in is pale shimmering gold. Imagine that golden light beginning to glow inside you and just be with that for a moment. Just feel. How would it be if that was in fact the truth?

Do this exercise as often as you think about it and certainly do it every time you start feeling small and useless and not enough. If you stick to just this one practical step you will find that it begins to change your reality, first in small ways and then in bigger ways until suddenly you do really begin to know that there is a Divine spark living right inside of you.

To reach that understanding is the hardest part of the journey. You may have to be quite pointed in the search and chip away ongoingly at the negativity and the chaos that keeps running interference to the concept of divinity. One day you will wake up and there will be more of you that can be in that space of divinity, more of you that is not fearful, more of you that is not anxious, more of you that trusts, more faith, more stepping into your true power. For every being it is the ultimate journey and what you need to know is that there are no unhappy endings. In the end every single human, every single living, breathing being in the Universe will remember that it is Divine. The journey there can be long and tedious, or simple and light, depending on how you want to make it. The trick is just to keep on keeping on.

You talk about stepping back into my Higher Self. How do I do that?

Stepping into your Higher Self is the easiest thing you can do. All you have to do is breathe it in. Nothing is solid, including you, and all you have to do is take a conscious breath, knowing that inside you and in the air around you is only divinity. The only thing you have to do is to be conscious of that and breathe, knowing that in that conscious breath you have just connected with your Divine self. All it takes is the acknowledgement of that. Just look up and take a deep breath. Try it in this moment and feel your energy field expanding and becoming brighter and notice yourself becoming lighter. The act of looking up connects you to the feeling of 'something else' which is why all cathedrals and holy places were built to great heights. Looking up connects you with the feeling of your soul and the light of the Divine.

If you consciously add a bit of truth and breathe in: "I am an ancient, powerful being of light" you will feel how every cell responds to that deep soul truth about you. The more you do that the more you get to live your soul's truth. Your soul always moves you away from fear and towards love. Fear is just your primate body thinking life is all about survival. Your

Higher Self knows it is eternal and nothing has ever happened that has not been for its highest good.

Your Higher Self is part of you and it is always there. It is your essence, it is who you really are. When you forget that it is your essence you have to consciously choose to open to hearing it and seeing it and feeling it. Here is an exercise, one of many taught to me by an amazing teacher called Jann Weiss, to help you step into your Higher Self.

Stand somewhere where you have space to step to your right. Now close your eyes and imagine that next to you, your Higher Self is beginning to create a 'you' that can hold fifty percent more of your Higher Self's energy. Feel the energy next to you beginning to buzz. Put your hand out and feel it. Can you feel it? Now step into it. Breathe it in. Can you feel how much lighter it is? Just stand there in the energy for a few seconds then step out of it back to your original position. Feel how different that feels. Now choose. Which energy will serve you best?

When you are ready step into that Higher you again, breathe it in and claim it: "I am this." From this position, now ask your Higher Self to create another 'you', able to hold even more of your soul's knowledge. Feel that 'you' being created next to you. Feel the energy begin to buzz. Put your hand out and feel it and when it feels complete, step into it. Feel the light expanding inside you. Feel your soul, your Higher Self's peace expanding inside you. Breathe it in. Stand there for a few seconds then step out of it, back as you were before. And choose. Which reality serves you best? Then step into the new reality. Claim it: "I Am this on the planet!" and then let your Higher Self remove the old you. That energy is gone. Now ask your Higher Self if there is anything more you need to know at this time. Be open to the information and when you are complete with it, open your eyes.

You can also simply remember, simply choose to know that your Higher Self is there and part of you. Open to hearing its voice – not your mother's voice that says you were never good enough or your father's voice that said you should have been better but your soul's voice which says you are perfect. If you stop listening to your mind talk instead what you will hear is the voice of love that has never ceased since time began. It has been whispering in your ear, in your mind and in your heart. It says you are perfect, you are Divine, you are loved; it says you need and lack nothing. It is there and you are it and it is you. It is the essence of who you are and there is no separation.

I wish I could get rid of my ego. I am trying so hard to live my life in a spiritual way and my ego keeps tripping me up. What can I do about it?

Your ego is not tripping you up. Your ego is the most important part of your spiritual journey. Without it you wouldn't have even considered taking the journey in the first place. The ego gives you the opportunity to experience yourself as a separate being and it helps you find the place within you where you recognise that you have value. That is the first step on your spiritual journey. The ego helps you fall in love with yourself enough to actually begin the journey back towards your divinity. If you had no ego you would not have taken the first step towards finding out what your Higher Self was and you would not have been able to conceive of the possibility that there was more to you than just your physical primate self. The difficulty comes if you stop the journey there and you then use your ego to flatten other people and that is really more about insecurity than ego. So do not fight your ego, use your ego as you would every other aspect of yourself and love it instead. Totally stop fighting it – in fact, stop fighting. What you resist persists. Really – don't fight your ego, love it. You can't fight anything right, you can only love it right and that is a universal truth that can be fitted into every single question ever in the history of the world. Not a single thing can be fought into submission.

The fight against the ego has been such a big misunderstanding. What you have difficulty with is often just disguised low self-esteem. When you see what you think is a rampant ego rolling around trying to take over the world, what you are looking at is a three year old yelling: "Look at me, look at me!!!" This often happens when a healthy sense of self has been squashed or denied somewhere along the line and now it desperately needs to be seen and heard but because it got stuck at the age of three, the behaviours you see are more like those of a three year old. Your ego is actually your friend. It shows you where all the buried patterns and blocks and issues sit and if you listen to what it is really saying, you will find that all anyone really wants, including you, is to be loved. Have compassion for that three year old who wasn't allowed to be noisy or bright or lazy or artistic or quiet or whatever it was in you that got squashed. Give it all the love it thought it never received and when it feels safe and loved it will no longer need to act out in quite such destructive ways.

Your real ego is a shiny bright yellow spark at the centre of your being that allows you to see your own "I". It is the part of you that is unique and amazing and special, the part of you that is like no one else on the planet, the part of you that has the opportunity to express all of that singular specialness that is only ever your own. If you did not have an ego you would never have considered going on a spiritual journey as you would not have known that you were special enough to go looking for 'more'. Dolphins have no ego so the pod-mind is what makes them do what they do. You are part of the whole too of course but you are also more than that. It is because of your ego that you are able to have your separate experiences and thoughts and in that, you feed incredibly special pieces of information back to the Allness.

The ideal is to make absolute best friends with your ego and let it show you what it knows about you as the amazing and wonderful human you are – and then take the extra step and release any judgement the church or anyone else taught you about what it means to have an ego. While you're in judgement about anything, including what you call ego, it keeps you from seeing the wonder of it and stops you from experiencing the useful and extraordinary qualities it has to offer.

How do I let go of judgement?

You become conscious of it – that is the key. When you notice yourself going into judgement, do whatever you need to do to get in touch with your Divine self because the minute you do that you will realise exactly what it is you are doing when you are judging and you will begin to look at it all from a completely different angle. If you look at the world and see a terrible place where so many awful things happen you will say how can you not judge that, how can you not judge murder, rape, theft, molestation? Those are BAD things! What if you could step out of that mindset? Could you shift your perspective, could you step out of the judgement, even for a moment, and ask: What if this really is an opportunity for someone to learn something? What if this thing really is an opportunity, what if it really is for the highest good? What if there is a higher picture here that that I am not aware of, that I cannot see from my space of judgement?

You do not ever judge anything unless it has something to do with you. You only judge it if it is in some way a mirror. You are never angry for the reason you think you are. When something rattles your cage and you find yourself in judgement and frustration and anger, if you sit with it you will always find it mirrors something in your life that you have yet to face or acknowledge or come to terms with. Once again it is an opportunity – an opportunity to be absolutely true and honest with yourself. When an outside event happens and you find yourself in judgement, stop and really get honest with yourself and you will see that there is something you have been carrying inside you which has not yet been dealt with. This event or thing that has happened which has thrown you off course is another opportunity to get clear, to be in impeccability, to find the piece inside that has not yet been acknowledged. You may not even realise you are holding on to it until something happens to reveal it to you. The key is that it is always your stuff. It is never about the other person.

The thing you judge is very often the thing you've never forgiven yourself for. If you are willing to face the unspeakable in yourself, those black spots inside you that you have been too scared to look at, you will discover that they are the very things you now judge the most. If you are prepared to go back to those places you will often see that whatever you are judging was something that happened to you when you were a child and you didn't know what to do with it. You may also find that you were the perpetrator of that very thing in a previous life. If you are in judgement of people you perceive as abusing the planet, ask yourself in which lifetime did you abuse it? If you cannot forgive the person who stole your partner away from you, when did you take something precious from someone? When you get angry with someone for being inconsiderate and ignoring your feelings, when did you do that to someone? Whatever you are now sitting in judgement of was set up so that your button could be pressed so that you could find the key inside yourself and forgive yourself – not the other, but yourself – and let go of the judgement.

The trick when you feel a judgement come up, when you go into fear or rage or frustration, is to look deeply into the place inside you where there is silence and ask to be shown the truth from a higher perspective. Follow the feelings all the way to the first time you can remember having them. Look back at your life and ask: "When did I first feel like this? How old was I when I first felt this way?" because it is often in your emotional body that the feeling sits. If you ask to be shown when the feeling first occurred in your life you will often get a sense or a memory or an insight into what triggered that feeling. When you get that, you can recognise that the anger and rage you are feeling is not actually anything to do with what is going on outside, that it was simply a trigger to get you to the unresolved feeling. It was set up for you so that the button could be pressed so that you could see the truth and get beyond the judgement and forgive yourself so that you could step into the perfection of each moment.

Show your Higher Self – that part of you who is vast and wise and so very, very loving, that part of you that is still completely connected to the Divine – show that part of you how it feels to be you. Go deeply into the feeling and really feel it again all the way down to the little child inside you and ask your Higher Self to come right into the feeling with you and it will help you transform that feeling. The higher vibration of your Higher

Self has the power to transform the lower vibration of any negative emotion. If you allow it to, your Higher Self can even transform that feeling into love.

When you let go of judgement you can open to a whole new world of gratitude and bliss and perfection in each moment. Do you really want to carry your judgements around? They only weigh heavily upon you. Would you not rather open to the true lightness of who you really are? Your judgements are not you. You are not your judgements. Let them go now. Put them down. Set them – and yourself – free.

I truly want to be of service. How can I help others?

Why do you want to be of service? Are you a servant? Why do others need your help? You see, you are not a body with a soul, you are a massive soul focusing through a tiny body. If that's the truth, your greatest service and gift and your reason for existing is to be in a clear space where you are totally living from your soul's perspective. By being in that space you remind others automatically, just by being you – and then they don't need your help. It is a joyous thing to be in a space with someone where you can see them remembering that they are the light but that is not 'helping' them, that is simply being and living your truth and watching the recognition response in everyone around you.

As a parent the greatest gift you can give your child is to be in your I Amness, your greatest Divine self and if you can extend that to everyone around you, that is your true service on the planet. It goes back to 'Namaste' – the Divine in me sees the Divine in you. The Divine in you is perfectly on track and on purpose, dealing with whatever it is that you have set up for your highest good. Honour and acknowledge that the Divine in the other person is also perfectly on track for their highest good and you will be of great service.

How do I hold a space for someone who is going through something difficult?

When you sit with someone who has just come through a massive shock you need to remember that they do not need you to immediately and judgementally ask: "So what did you do to create that??" In that moment they need you to offer compassion and sweet tea. When you start tapping into the place inside you where the answers live, always remember that your main job is still to practice compassion even if you can see clearly where the person went off track so that they needed to be shocked back onto their path. All the time, the only way is compassion and true deep empathy for the ones coming up behind you. If you can always remember to treat yourself and everyone else with complete love you will find that you can also manage to treat them with complete understanding.

Move into your Divine self and insist on seeing the Divine in the other person. You cannot drop them if you are insisting on seeing the Divine in them. What you are seeing is only God experiencing. There is nothing else going on. If someone is in their stuff and you are insisting on seeing them as God, going through their stuff, there is nothing more you need to do. It is a kind of 'so what?' energy, but this is not a judgemental 'so what?' it is a fully compassionate state of being. The key then is to apply this to yourself. Hold this space for yourself. Insist on seeing the Divine in yourself in every moment.

What do I do when I really need to understand why something has happened in order to make peace with it?

In the moment of shock or pain when something happens in your life you deal with the event because it is right in front of you and requires your attention, whether it makes sense to you or not. Invariably there will come a time later when you can look at the event again and unpick the threads until you realise that it was exactly the shock that pushed you into a different direction or that created exactly the right moment to meet someone that you would otherwise not have connected with. Truly, there is always, always a reason for every event – those you call good and those you label bad. Nothing is random. Everything is always precisely and mathematically perfect but the problem is that on a conscious level you do not always know the how or the why. It is your vast Higher Self which knows why things really happen and because in the past you have successfully cut yourself off from that higher guidance, you had to rely instead on faith and trust. If you can stay in a conscious state of love all the time you will find that the answers to your questions will be easier to access. You will find that the answers are there right under the love. The more you stay connected to that higher guidance, the less important it becomes to know 'why' something happened. You just know that it was the perfect experience for the perfect reason to get you wherever you need to be right now.

How do I learn from a situation so that I can resolve it?

This question says you are already taking such a huge step in the right direction. You are not blaming the situation or person. You are looking at the world as an opportunity to heal and learn. From that space it is quite easy then to look at the situation and see that it teaches you compassion, it teaches you how to love at a deeper level, it teaches you how to not blame, it teaches you all sorts of things. In this question is a person who already is on the right path, already looking at an event as an opportunity – and that is stunning! It is a beautiful, beautiful question and it certainly comes from a place where the world can work, because that is exactly the energy you need to take into every situation. If you can be very clear that every situation is there to help you heal, to teach you, to get you back to the light, then the whole process becomes such an elegant, easy, clear way to do life on this planet.

This question shows that you are ready to do life in a new way and the new way that is being presented to you is to find a very narrow road and not stray from it. You are asked to wake up every morning and know that everything that is presented to you is for your highest good. If you can totally 'know' in the cells of your being that every single event and moment in the whole day is there for your benefit, then you are never going to judge where you are as a difficult situation that is teaching you a hard lesson. Do you understand the difference? If you are walking in wide-eyed expectation through your day and you bump up against a flat tyre, you are not going to wail and cry, "Why me, why now..?" You are going to take a deep breath and look for the gift and expect to meet your soul mate when they stop to help you change your tyre. You are not going to even notice that life is presenting you with difficulties. You are going to look at every event as an opportunity to have the most wonderful moment of your life. You are going to start digging like the little boy who was given a pile of horse manure because with so much manure there had to be a pony.

At this point you have moved very far from playing at spirituality. You are now being asked to be a true spiritual adult and that means that you do not judge or give labels to anything. You just know that everything simply is. You can be in the midst of a war and know that it is another human construct for the greatest good. Yes, it would be fun to instantly know the reason why something is in your reality but if you stay neutral and completely in your I Amness you do not even really need to know. Needing answers is just another way to try and tell the Divine how to run the Universe: "OK God, tell me why you did that and I will tell you if you if you did the right thing."

The more you are able to tune into the Divine knowing within you, the more you will be in the flow and the more you will be in a space where you do not need anything to be different because you will constantly be tapping into the perfection unfolding. Your very being will be so in resonance to what is, that there will not be any stress and pain. It is very hard to imagine if you are in pain and in stress right now, but pain and stress are not part of your natural state. They are learned behaviours because of the initial judgement that the world and humanity were imperfect things created by an imperfect Creator. Sit just where you are and take a very deep breath and feel if that is the truth. In the silence you will find the truth. Just be in this moment fully and feel. What is, right at this moment, not perfect? You are alive. You are breathing. Do not go to what was not perfect yesterday and what will not be perfect tomorrow. Just this moment. Feel the perfection of this moment, and then the next, and the next. Practice this all the time and keep bringing yourself back to this moment until you can begin to feel a long line of perfect moments stretching out ahead and behind you. Then look back and really acknowledge that every moment up to this one brought you here and so they were perfect and if that is the truth, all the rest of the moments of your life will also be perfect.

Why does enlightenment seem like such hard work?

When has anything worthwhile ever been easy on this planet? Here it is all struggle and hard work and enlightenment is the most worthwhile thing that exists so it figures that it would also be the most difficult – right?

Well, yes, and not so much. It really is exactly what you expect it to be. If you believe that life is hard and you must struggle to reach an enlightened state then that is exactly what you will experience. If you are lucky enough to know the truth that you are a Divine being who is on the planet to remember who you are and that the outcome is blissful, then it will not be hard. In each moment you can choose what you want to experience. In reality all it takes is to be mindful in each moment and to choose with each breath – but it does take that much focus. Each and every breath has to be a choice to breathe in more of your I Amness and more of your soul. Enlightenment means living your soul's vote in your physical body. Are you nervous? Body's vote. Are your shoulders tight? Body's vote. Fearful? Body's vote. Horrified by the way people treat children or animals? Body's vote... Your job is to stay focused and aware of how much of your day you are running on the body's vote and how much you are able to live from your soul's vote. Blissful feelings? Soul. Love of everything? Soul. Detached compassion? Soul.

If you want to reach an enlightened state it has to be what you want more than you want to breathe. When you want enlightenment more than you want life then it is easy because you will let nothing stand in your way. Your focus will be one-pointed and you will practice like a concert soloist – all the hours that you are given. You will not let yourself be distracted. If you ask a master musician if playing the violin is difficult he will probably say that it is the most difficult thing and the easiest. Enlightenment is exactly like that but unlike the concert violinist, who needs talent as well as hard work, the journey toward enlightenment just takes choice and concentration. You just have to want it and go for it and the more you experience the blissful moments the more you will do to experience them again. When you realise how much you are also adding to everything else on the planet when you are in bliss, you will realise that moving toward enlightenment is the most important thing any human can ever do. So please, for your own sake and for all of the planet's sake, keep your focus and do not get discouraged. Remember that there is no 'there' that you are actually striving for. You are already enlightened. You are already enlightenment. Your job is simply to keep being willing to move to the next level of awareness.

How do I expand my consciousness?

You expand your consciousness by doing it. Not by trying to do it. By being it. By wanting it. The thing is actually not to remember but to want, to seek, because the moment you ask the question, it opens the door. Keep talking to the God within you. Keep the connection. Keep knowing that it is there and just do it. Do it and be it.

You expand your consciousness by moving from fear to love. Fear is the part of the light that has had the biggest impact in pretending not to be the light and because it was so intriguing you had to go and play there for a while. You experienced fear so that you would know everything that is the light but because the fear was so intense and 'real' and because you liked the drama, you played in the fear for longer than you needed to – or not.

If you have chosen fear you have done so for your own purpose. How would it be not to judge the fear? How would it be to let the fear be the light in a fearful form with no added weight, with no added judgement? If you are experiencing fear at any time just be in it and feel it until it becomes something you no longer desire to feel and then lift yourself back out of fear into the light. Allow the fear to be what it is rather than fighting it. Why would you fight the light in its fearful form? Why would you not allow all of it? The moment you judge anything you are living a lie. Just be conscious. You can choose to live in a lie or in the light or you can do both. In doing both you get the opportunity to choose. Which makes your heart sing? Both are just experiences, for your highest good, because that is all that exists. There is not a lowest good or an in-between good, there is only a highest good because that is what is. It is so simple that you have not been able to believe it.

Third dimensional reality has been based on making up stories about everything and that has been a fascinating project and it has given you the opportunity to have experiences to be and do and play and manifest. Now you can choose to come back to the truth of the light or you can make up more stories. There is no end to time, no end to anything. It all unfolds just as it needs to. The light expands and contracts, it breathes out and in, it lives and moves. Now you have the opportunity to move beyond the limitations of a third dimensional life and it is your constant moment-by-moment choice to be present and to judge nothing that shifts your consciousness toward the light more than anything else you can do.

Why does the spiritual journey have to be so serious?

Ascension is a by-product of joy. If you cannot find the joy, if you will not allow yourself the joy, you cannot lift your vibration and raise your consciousness to a higher level. While you are sitting in the belief that life is serious and you think your job is to suffer, the Ascension process is not working. The Catholics already tried that with the idea that you had to struggle and suffer and crawl on glass and wear hair shirts and all the other little tortures they thought up. That is not the path to Ascension. Ascension is when you are in a place of: "Ahhhh, I love it here and the sun is shining!" That lifts the energy for the whole planet in ways you cannot imagine. One drop of joy changes masses of earnestness and seriousness.

Have you looked at your world lately? Have you noticed the beauty in everything around you? Have you seen what grows in your garden or along your road? Have you noticed the colours in the eye of the fly buzzing against your window? The Divine is one huge, smiling, loving energy and that is what focuses through you. If you are taking any of it seriously, you have removed yourself from your core. Your core energy is love and fun and joy. Notice what happens when you get all serious about your path and your mission and healing the world and feel just how much judgement is going on there. Now notice how your body feels when you step into the feeling of loving and enjoying life, of playing and having a wonderful time. Notice how your energy levels rise and your heart expands and your shoulders drop. If you're struggling to see how being happy can add to the world just take a look at the world from a higher viewpoint. Look down on the earth and see where all the struggle and contraction and seriousness happens and how the light there is dimmed, if you can see it at all. Now look at where all the points of love and laughter and joy are. Are they not the brightest, most magnificent points of light?

Where has the magic gone and how do we get it back?

The way to find the magic is to find the passion. Magic and passion are really almost the same thing because when you passionately follow a path, something magical happens. When you are passionate it is like being newly in love, it feels utterly magical and your reality reflects that. Everything is brighter, everything is shinier, everything tastes better, everything smells better, there is magic in the air. If there is nothing you are passionate about, if you haven't found what you are here to do, here is a key: Your essence self knows that it incarnated to find your passion, it incarnated because it knew that there was something or many things that you would be passionate about, it knew that there would be a path or paths that you would follow with passion. So go back to who you are in essence, go back to who is at the core of you, and once you really experience that and step into it, you will be able to access the knowing inside you of all the things that bring you passion and joy and that is where the magic happens. It only comes from the depth of the true you and when you find it, it feels like grace.

If you ever feel as if the magic has gone, as if you can't find it, remember that it is where you left it – in the depth of your soul. You are the magic but to get to it you have to be it. Sit with your head on your chest looking down and wrap your arms around yourself and see if you can find anything positive to focus on. You will soon realise that it is very difficult not to feel miserable in that position. Now fling your arms wide and lift your face up to the sky and look up and try and think of a problem. You will find that it is very difficult to be sad in that position. There is the magic! Your amazing physical form is capable of creating all the magic you need right there and once you have opened your body up and lifted your head and flung your arms out, do a twirl. You will almost instantly realise that you have gone from miserable to happy and you did that by simply changing your position. Now breathe "I Am" into your solar plexus and feel that light expanding and spread that light as far as you can and keep breathing and spreading that light and feel how the room lights up around you. Keep going for as long as you would like to and now tell me, where has the magic gone...?

And Finally....

What is it we're really doing here?

You are doing what you've always done. You are following the light, you are being the light and the light takes you where it needs you and whether you love it or resist it, there is only one thing and it is the light. You cannot not do the work of the light because nothing else exists. There is nothing outside of it. There is the opposite and that is the heavy, but that is also an aspect of the light. There is nothing that is not the One and you are it and it is you and there is no separation.

How do you know when you are following the light? The light feels light, the light is light. Your feelings are there to show you. Whether you are lightly being the light or heavily being the light there is no judgement on either path, it is simply the choice you make. You can do it with joy and laughter and love and lightness or you can love the drama and do it with imagined pain and suffering and difficulty and tragedy or whatever else you choose. The truth is, you cannot get it wrong. You have never got it wrong. There is only the light and you cannot step out of it. Hitler was the light and Saddam Hussein was the light and every monstrous thing you can imagine on the planet is the light expanding. Incredibly brave choices were made for the light to have the opportunity to experience everything that exists, everything that could be imagined. Humans were made to be everything and 'everything' cannot just be one aspect. Every part of creation looks like a disco ball, reflecting everything that exists all the time and you will focus on the part that reflects you in any given moment. You will be a reflection of the light of where your consciousness or your choices have brought you. You are endlessly creating all the time. Mostly in the past you have created from an unconscious place and part of what you are doing now is remembering how to create from consciousness instead of unconsciousness.

Everything you have ever experienced is registered in your brain. The brain is a microcosm of the macrocosm of the Universe. It is all there, accessible to you, and when you remember, it is there and you can access it. When you are busy playing at forgetting, notice that you can choose instead to play at remembering and you will once again find that it is all there, all available. If you meditated instead of googling you would have access to much more of the truth. If you used your true telepathic powers you would not need the internet; if you remembered how to bi-locate you would not have to pay for plane tickets; and if you used your energy to truly set Ascension in motion you would not need a microwave. What you have been looking for in the Hall of Records is within you. Everything that exists is within you. You are a cell in the body of God. If you expand your consciousness and expand it some more you begin to realise that the distance between cells is like the distance between the stars and that what looks solid is entirely an illusion and then you can be the space between the cells, the space between the stars. Even the concept of remembering loses it reality, its meaning. It is just being. Just is-ness. That is you and that is what you are really doing here.

About the Author

In 2001 Melissie Jolly created the Colour Mirrors system of colour therapy and now spends her time running workshops and producing the coloured oils and essences that make up the system. She lives in Stanford in the Western Cape, close to the southernmost tip of Africa. She has no idea how she got so lucky. Melissie was born in Kenya and emigrated with her parents as a small child to South Africa. She studied psychology and art before discovering that colour was her joy. She has three deeply adored children and a beloved little grandson.

Visit her website at www.colourmirrors.com.

Made in the USA
Charleston, SC
09 March 2015